Cricket
Back in time

This book is dedicated to both the past, my mother and

father, Agnes and Joseph and to the future, my children,

Lara and Andrew.

ACKNOWLEDGEMENTS

There are many people whom I would like to thank for their help in the writing and
publishing of this book: Fiona Schultz, Martin Ford, Linda Bottari and Leigh Nankervis at
New Holland Publishers, Mark Gilbert, Alan Whiticker, Karl Roper and Tony Burgess.
My sincere thanks to Bill Brown who consented to provide the foreword for this book,
and finally to my wife Erika, for her invaluable help right through this project.

First published in Australia in 2006 by
New Holland Publishers (Australia) Pty Ltd
Sydney • Auckland • London • Cape Town

14 Aquatic Drive Frenchs Forest NSW 2086 Australia
218 Lake Road Northcote Auckland New Zealand
86 Edgware Road London W2 2EA United Kingdom
80 McKenzie Street Cape Town 8001 South Africa

10 9 8 7 6 5 4 3 2 1

ISBN: 174110 4602

A record of this title is available from the National Library of Australia

Publisher: Fiona Schultz
Managing Editor: Martin Ford
Designer: Leigh Nankervis
Production: Linda Bottari
Printer: Tien Wah Press

Front Cover photos: Keith Miller; The Sydney Cricket Ground in 1959
Back Cover Photo: W.G.Grace's XI in 1899

PICTURE CREDITS

Special thanks to those who kindly made their photographic
material available.

All images courtesy of the Ian Collis Library and New
Holland Publishers, except for:
Gilbert, Mark Library: 19, 20b, 28t, 28b, 42br, 44t, 44b, 45t,
45b, 49t, 54/55, 63t, 80b, 84t, 88r, 90, 91l, 98tl, 98tr, 99t, 99b,
102t, 102b, 103t, 103m, 106/107, 109, 114t, 116t, 116b, 120tl,
120tr, 120/121, 121tr, 122tl, 123t, 148t, 148bl, 158b, 159, 170,
173, 189, 318.

News Limited: 215r, 223b, 300t, 312t, 313t, 315tr, 321, 322l,
324, 332, 340t, 340b, 343b, 344t, 344lb, 344/345b, 345t, 346t,
349tl, 349tr, 349b, 351, 352, 353t, 353b, 354t, 354b, 356,
357b.

Abbreviations: t = top, m = middle, b = bottom, l = left, r
= right

Cricket
Back in time

Ian Collis

NEW HOLLAND

Foreword

WILLIAM ALFRED BROWN *was born on 31 July, 1912 and at age 94 at the time of publication of this book, is Australia's oldest Test cricketer. Queensland-born (Toowoomba), Brown moved to Sydney with his family when he was four years old. A Marrickville junior, Bill Brown made his first class debut for NSW in the summer of 1932-33 — an historic time in Australian cricket, with the tour by Douglas Jardine's England team in the infamous 'Bodyline' series — and made his Test debut in 1934.*

A right-hand opening batsmen, Brown made his Test debut against England on the 1934 Ashes tour. He appeared in 22 Tests during his career and scored 1592 runs at an average of 46.82 with a top score of 206 not out. Brown scored over 13000 runs in his first class career and shared his memories of the champion players and great matches of the 1930s and 1940s exclusively for this book.

I didn't play in the 'Bodyline' series of 1932 but I did watch it. Douglas Jardine was a formidable character who never took a backward step. He was given a rough time out here but stood up to it fairly well. He set the world on fire with the Bodyline series but he also took the criticism and never gave way to what he believed.

Harold Larwood (England fast bowler) had a smooth run up and was quicker that anyone else at that time, although 'Gubby' Allen and Bill Voce were close. Allen didn't approve of Bodyline and refused to bowl it. Voce was an awkward bowler to face because he bowled a lot of short stuff at you. He bowled left arm round the wicket very quickly with the ball aimed into the body. He was a strong man and just kept at you.

I was first selected for Australia on the 1934 tour of England. Playing with Bill Woodfull, Don Bradman, Stan McCabe and Bill Ponsford was a wonderful experience for a scrubber like me. I could see what made them great players was because each were unique in their own way. Woodfull was a great team man and leader, and Bradman was the finest batsman I have ever seen.

The boat trip to England was all fun and no hard work. We had a steward to look after us— run a batch, lay clothes out on bed etc. It was 'black tie' every night for dinner. (Australian all-rounder) Hans Ebeling had a beautiful voice … Woodfull would make him sing in the dressing room after a match and we would all join in. Bill would say, 'A team that sings together is a happy team.' In Swansea, Wales we heard a wonderful harmony coming from the Welsh dressing room. Our singing died away after that and we never sang again.

The 1930s was a great time. During the tour Joe Darling would say, 'Every night is carnival night.' After World War II, there were no more 'black tie' nights.

I moved to Brisbane in 1936 and represented Queensland in the Sheffield Shield competition. That year (against England in the fourth Test in Adelaide) Stan McCabe played one of the finest innings I have ever seen.

He was an orthodox player, but with such power and precision. After McCabe came in to the dressing room exhausted after his great innings (88) Bradman said, 'If I could ever play an innings like that, I would be a happy man.' (Bradman went out and scored 270 in the second innings of the match).

Don Bradman lifted your game and you tried to follow him. He was so much better than everyone else of his era. He inspired you to lift your own game. He was responsible for some of the success you had because you tried to emulate him … but when you played with him, you knew he was the best.

Len Hutton (England opener and captain) was another player with a wonderful technique — all scoring shots and no wild ones. When Hutton scored 364 (in the fifth Test of the 1937-38 Ashes series at the Oval) I was fielding about six to eight feet away on the leg side with Len batting and 'Tiger' Bill O'Reilly bowling at him. I stood there for about three days until 'Tiger' got him out.

364 runs … it was something I didn't think I could aspire to. In the next match of the tour I scored a career best 260 not out against Derbyshire.

Bill O'Reilly was one of the great figures of international cricket. Batsmen were his chief enemy and he took to them accordingly … when he bowled he was preceded down the wicket by waves of hostility, as batsman expected. He had a wonderful 'wrong-un' and leg break. He had the ability to turn the ball the other way and got great bounce. Don Bradman said that Bill was the greatest bowler he ever faced.

After World War II, I resumed my playing career against Test newcomers New Zealand (1946) and India (1947–48). Walter Hadlee, the Kiwi captain was a really fine fellow. New Zealand won the toss in the only Test played and decided to bat. I don't know why? They only got 42 and 54 in each innings.

The 1948 'Invincibles' was a wonderful Australian team — Sid Barnes, Arthur Morris, Lindsay Hassett, Ian Johnson, Neil Harvey, Sam Loxton, Don Tallon, Keith Miller, Ray Lindwall, Bill Johnston and, of course, Don Bradman. 'The Don' was the best on-field captain I ever played with. He had his fast bowlers fresh and ready when he needed them.

The most inspiring captain I played under was Vic Richardson. The boys in the team loved him. He was the first man up in the morning and the last one to go to bed. Vic never asked you to do anything he wouldn't do himself. (Australian cricketer) Arthur Jones said to Arthur Chipperfield that he couldn't play one day because he felt sick; had a headache and felt dizzy. Vic Richardson said to him, 'Come down and play, I feel like that every morning.'

So many great names … regarding wicketkeepers, Don Tallon and Bert Oldfield were great wicketkeepers. Tallon was arguably the best wicketkeeper I played with during my career. Jack Fingleton, I have the greatest respect for. Keith Miller was a natural athlete; he had a great pair of hands and was a wonderful bowler and attacking batsman. Keith and Ray Lindwall were a formidable pair of bowlers. Lindwall had a wonderful action … a smooth run up and delivery with complete control of the ball. He had great speed and always knew where he was going to bowl.

This cricket book takes us through a journey of remembrance from the earliest days of the game until the 'new era' of one-day cricket. Not only those who remember earlier times, but youngsters who only know the new game, will enjoy this book of magnificent photos. Ian Collis has painstakingly researched this photographic history, not only of cricketers of their time, but also the spectators, venues and times. Books such as this are an important part of keeping the history of our game alive.   April 2006

Contents

Introduction

by Ian Collis

AS AN HISTORIAN, I have always searched for the origins and images of our past, be it our way of life, our culture, our growth and our pastimes. What made us happy, how did we dress, how did we live, what was our mode of transport and how did our city and way of life evolve? I have been searching for those 'moments' now for over 30 years: forever looking for 'that shot' which captured our heritage.

For the sports and cricket enthusiast of the past, there was no television, no replay of every controversial incident, no super slow motion or any of the other technology that is available today. If you wanted to watch a game of international cricket you went to the ground, or if that was not possible, listened to it on the radio or read about it in the evening or morning newspapers. In this regard the sports photographer was all-important. He had to try and capture the 'moment' that told the story of the match.

Many photographers, their names now lost in history, took photos that never saw the light of day — or if they did, only for a fleeting moment on the back page of a daily newspaper. They were lost for decades; collecting dust in corners of newspaper or publishing libraries or zealously collected and guarded by memorabilia hunters and sports lovers alike. Through years of searching and gathering I have managed to locate many 'gems' that, when put together in chronological order, tell a wonderful story of cricket and cricketers through the generations. From the late 1800s right through to the cricketing revolution of the 1970s, a story told by visual image can now be shown. And just as the old saying goes, 'a picture tells a thousand words'.

> *The game of cricket transcends all levels of talent — from the gifted to the not so gifted; from the legendary to the anonymous*

Cricket has been played from the very early days of British history in some form or other. It has been a source of great enjoyment to many a youth who aspired to captain his country or just to be part of a team in a park somewhere. The game of cricket transcends all levels of talent — from the gifted to the not so gifted; from the legendary to the anonymous. But most importantly, it is a game to be enjoyed by the masses ... a national pastime.

From the game's earliest days, right through to the mid 1970s, the leading players were treated like royalty by a devoted public who could only dream of emulating similar deeds on the playing fields. When we recall cricket played in the mists of time, we think of one name ... Bradman. Statistics say he was the best; yet there were many who came before him, who also excelled at this sport. And there were 'heroes' galore. From the days of the imperious Englishman Dr. W.G.Grace, to the 1930s and '40s when the Australian Don Bradman reigned supreme, through to the brilliant West Indian all-rounder Garfield Sobers of the 1960s and '70s.

This book is presented in seven main chapters. Each chapter looks at the characters and matches in that era. The first chapter covers the era from the very beginning of Test cricket, when in 1877 England met Australia in Melbourne through to the 1909 season, when the M.A.Noble led Australians faced A.C.Maclaren's Englishmen. Test cricket was played by but a few nations, with England, Australia and South Africa the participants. The following chapter then covers the period just before and after the Great War. And when Test cricket resumed in 1920–21 some had been lost forever in far away battles. And in 1928 and 1929 the West Indies and New Zealand teams celebrated their Test inclusion with their first series against England. The thirties was a mixture of the very best (Bradman), the most controversial tour of all (Bodyline) and the delight of India gaining test status. The highlight of the forties is Bradman leading his 'Invincibles' on a tour to England. Finally into the later decades, from the fifties through to the seventies, the emergence of some the best cricketers from around the world is captured.

Packer had the means and know-how and grabbed the game by the scruff of the neck

While as long as the game had been played the best of the best would always rise to the top, generation after generation, and one thing had remained the same. Cricket was seen as a game — not a profession; no matter how much the administrator's coffers were swollen by the full houses that were turning up to watch them perform. The players were paid, but compared to the takings accumulated through the gate it just didn't seem a fair system of remuneration. Finally, the game came to the crossroads in the mid 1970s. Cricket officialdom was dismayed by the players' demands … after all, cricket was a game and if you didn't want to play there was always someone else happy to take your spot. It had been the same for over 100 years.

Before the 'revolution', cricket was a different game; there were few one-day internationals, sparse advertising on the perimeters of grounds, no coloured clothing and no sponsor logos on the field. Cricket was a game played by gentlemen and the 'Test Match' was the ultimate contest. And the ultimate prize was the 'Ashes' trophy — a small terracotta urn holding the ashes of burnt cricket stumps — which has been the source of Anglo-Australian sporting endeavour for over a hundred years.

In 1977, the cricket world was turned upside down by a man named Kerry Packer. The Australian media mogul had heard the frustrations of the leading players of the time — headed by Ian Chappell's Australian team — who just wanted a 'better deal'. Packer had the means (wealth) and know-how (business) and grabbed the game by the scruff of the neck and gave it an almighty shake. This is where our photographic journey finishes. The 'new game' as we now know it was ready to be taken forward, but this book is a celebration of those who came before.

For those who can still remember watching cricket on television in flickering images in black and white — and just as importantly, for those fans of the game who came after the 'revolution' — this book is another chance to look back, to remember and learn about the history of the game.

Cricket Back in Time is a book for all generations — not just the old — and will be enjoyed by those who love the game, no matter what age. Many of the images have never before been seen or published. These rare photographs take us through a journey from the days before we came together as a nation, through to the year the game changed forever.

Take a stroll through Australia's sporting history; enjoy those long ago times, the people and the fashions … and the great cricketing moments captured, and now preserved, for all time.

The Origins
of Cricket

WHILE THE ORIGINS OF CRICKET ARE CLOUDED, we do know that the game was played in England in some form as far back as the 12th Century. However the game that we see played today would be a far cry from the quaint pastime enjoyed in those far off days. References to cricket matches can be found in artworks and etchings, and the works of historians in the centuries leading up to 1700. The venues for the playing of this early form of the game were often churchyards and village greens. The game that was played then would have been 'for frivolity' — but it was still quite a dangerous pastime. In 1624 in Sussex, fielder Jaspar Vinall was killed as the batsman swung at the ball a second time to avoid being caught.

The first conclusive records for a game recognisable as cricket describe a match played in Kent in 1646. The first match between English counties was played between Surrey and Kent at Dartford Brent on 29 June, 1709. With the early enthusiasm for the sport shown by the upper class in England, the game spread to Cambridge and Oxford schools in the early part of the 18th Century. Cricket was taking a foothold in the culture of the country and the sub-conscious of its peoples. And the game grew in popularity; it was played by wealthy gentlemen, at public schools, in villages, and even foreign territories, notably India, where mariners of the East India Company were spreading the virtues of the game, and of course England's newest colony … New South Wales.

In England, Thomas Lord (1755–1832) was employed by the White Conduit Club after the members decided to found the 'Marylebone Cricket Club'. The MCC soon became the pre-eminent cricket power of the land and, as for Thomas Lord, his name would last forever at 'Lords', the home of English and international cricket. The first book of cricket 'instruction' was published in 1801. The cover stated that: 'Rules & Instructions for playing at the game of cricket, as practiced by the most eminent players. To which is subjoined the laws and regulations of cricketers, as revised by the Cricket Club at Mary-le-bone'.

By 1805, the year of the Battle of Trafalgar, top-hats were the cricketer's chosen headgear (though fashionable, it must be noted that they were not as safe as the head gear worn by the modern cricketer). The Duke of Wellington, who watched his troops play cricket near Brussels prior to the Battle of Waterloo (1815), is alleged to have said that the battle was really won on the playing fields of Eton … and many a patriotic cartoonist dwelt on this assertion.

ABOVE W.G.Grace's X1 versus the Australians at Crystal Palace Park, London in July, 1899. In the foreground, left to right is: L.C.Braund (tall player with dark cap), W.G.Quaife, W.G.Grace and F.Martin.

The early games, in some parts, were referred to as a merely 'manly diversion'. In most quarters it was regarded as a pastime for men only, and certain types of men at that. But women would not be excluded, and in a few short years an end-of-season 'contest' between women offered huge prize money. In 1811 it was noted that: 'a grand female cricket match between 11 of Surrey and 11 of Hampshire, made by two noblemen, for 500 Guineas, will be played at the late Robert Thornton, Esq's Park, near the plough, Clapham.'

In 1821 Lachlan Macquarie, the Governor of New South Wales, instructed his storekeeper to order some cricket bats and balls for scholars at the local academy. More seeds of the game of cricket were thus planted in another corner of the Empire.

Action from the Fourth Test match at the SCG between Stoddardt's English team against G Giffen's Australian side in 1895. Although

1877 – 1909

1

1877

Although the Aboriginals were the first Australian representative team to play the MCC in England, the matches were not given 'Test' status

THE FIRST MATCH BETWEEN AN 11-MAN MCC TEAM representing England and 15 players (reduced from 22 when the visitors complained of exhaustion after their two month trip to Australia) representing the Australian colony of Victoria was played at the MCG on New Years Day, 1862. The English tour was sponsored by Melbourne hoteliers Felix Spiers and Christopher Pond and were led by Heathfield Harman Stephenson, the captain of Surrey. Although some of the MCC matches against various XXII's were referred to as 'Tests' the only first class match played was between members of the England team (Surrey) and a group of local players and spare tourists (The World) in March.

George Parr led England's second tour of Australia in 1863-64. The MCC team also played a Victorian XXII at the MCG on New Years Day, 1864 and later appeared in three matches against NSW in Sydney's Domain. Following the departure of the MCC, cricket was the most popular sport in Australia. The game was even played on the cattle stations, pastoral 'squatting lands' and aboriginal missions in the Western Districts of Victoria. An Aboriginal team was formed in the summer of 1866-67 with seven of the players forming the nucleus of the first Australian tour of England in 1868. Apart from Johnny 'Mullagh', who scored 1698 runs and took 245 wickets, 'Cuzens' and Charles Lawrence, who led the team, the performances of the rest of the team were quite poor (W.G.Grace described them as 'boomerangers and spear throwers rather than cricketers.') 'King Cole' died of tuberculosis on tour and Sundown and Jim Crow were sent home ill — leaving the remaining 11 players to finish the tour without substitution. Although the Aboriginals were the first Australian representative team to play the MCC in England, the matches were not given 'Test' status and the deeds of the fourteen players are not included in official Cricket records.

England's third tour to Australia in 1873–74, saw the great man William Gilbert Grace (1848–1915) as part of the team; albeit also using the trip as a well-paid honeymoon. In any sport, you can only truly judge how good a player is by how they fare against their opponents of that era. Grace, as Bradman would prove many years later, was a class above his contemporaries in every regard.

The arrival of James Lillywhite's MCC team in 1876–77 resulted in the birth of Anglo-Australian Test cricket on March 15, 1877. The Australian XI won the match at the MCG by 45 runs after opener Charles Bannerman scored 165 runs. Few, in Australia at least, care to recall that England won the second Test by 4 wickets to square the two-Test series, but the locals' success eventually led to an invitation to travel to England in 1878.

Ten years after the Aboriginal tour of England, the first full-scale Australian team, led by Dave Gregory, travelled to England after exhibition matches in Brisbane, Sydney, Melbourne and New Zealand. Only 12 players went on the tour, leaving no room for injury, illness or poor form. The Australians thrashed the MCC at Lords by 10 wickets, but it was hardly worthy of an international match, let alone a 'Test'. England crumbled with scores of 33 and 19, while Australia fared only marginally better with 41 — requiring just 12 runs for victory.

Australia won the only Test played during England's tour of 1878–79. In the first week of January, 1879, Australia thrashed the MCC by 10 wickets after Fred Spofforth captured 13 wickets for 110, which included a hat-trick (not surprisingly, the first hat-trick in Test history) in the first innings. (A second Test planned for Sydney was abandoned after a riot during the England v NSW match). The 1880 Australian team became the first team to play a Test match on English soil. Billy Murdoch top-scored with 153 in this match (beating W.G.Grace's score of 152) but the home-side won the Test by 5 wickets.

> *The 1880 Australian team became the first team to play a Test match on English soil.*

The England team that sailed to Australia and New Zealand as part of the Shaw/Shrewsbury/Lillywhite enterprise in 1881–82 was racked by bribery and betting allegations. The first Test in Melbourne was drawn but the 'colonials' had the final say on the troubled tour when they won consecutive Tests in Sydney.

The only Test played on Australia's tour of England in 1882 at The Oval, proved to be one of the most famous matches in Anglo-Australian sporting history. The man chiefly responsible for Australia's upset victory was 'The Demon' Fred Spofforth with figures of 7/46 and 7/44. Australia's demoralising win in two days was the catalyst for a mock obituary of English cricket by Reginald Shirley Brooks in the *Sporting Times* on the following Saturday, September 2, 1882.

> *In Affectionate Remembrance of ENGLISH CRICKET, which died at the Oval on 29th AUGUST, 1882. Deeply lamented by a large circle of sorrowing friends and acquaintances R.I.P.*
>
> *N.B. — The body will be cremated and the ashes taken to Australia.*

In the two decades before the end of 19th Century, Australia and the MCC hosted biannual 'Ashes' Test series (in 1888 two England teams toured Australia, but only one Test was played, which England won in Sydney). In 1900–01, Australia retained the Ashes won in England in 1899. Archie MacLaren led the last tour of Australia by a privately managed team, but the Englishmen slumped to lose the last three Tests of the series after the series was evenly poised at one Test each. Clem Hill (who topped 500 runs in the series without making a century) and bowlers 'Monty' Noble and Hugh Trumble starred in Australia's 4–1 Test series win.

1909

1877

Joe Darling captained Australia on the 1902 Ashes Tour of England. The first Test at Edgbaston looked well and truly won when England bowled Australia out for 36 after declaring at 9/376. However, the elements that conspired to bring Australia to its knees in their first innings (Victor Trumper top-scored with just 18 while the other ten batsmen failed to make double figures) ultimately denied England a victory. The visitors retained the Ashes with an historic win at Old Trafford in the fourth Test. Opener Victor Trumper scored a century before tea on the first day of play but England looked set to tie the series when they bowled Australia out for 86 in the second innings. Needing just 124 for victory, Frank Tate was last man out for England — bowled three runs short in the closest Test match result on record. England won the fifth Test of the series — by 1 wicket — but the Ashes (figuratively, at least) were on their way back to Australia.

In 1902–03, less than two years after the end of the Boer War, an Australian cricket team traveled to South Africa for the first time. However, the following year, Australia's run of four consecutive Ashes series wins finally ended in defeat. In the first official MCC tour of Australia, the first Test showcased the talents of England's R.E.Foster (287) and Victor Trumper (185) but by the vital fourth Test, the visitors held a 2–1 advantage. England captain 'Plum' Warner threatened to take his team from the SCG because of the noisy crowd demonstrations when Clem Hill was run out but Australian captain 'Monty' Noble appealed for calm and England ultimately won the match — and the Ashes.

England retained the Ashes in 1905, with captain F.S.Jackson topping both the batting (492 runs at 70.28) and bowling (13 wickets at 15.46) averages. Australia was beaten by 'Bosie's (Bernard Bosanquet) googlies' in England, losing the Test series 2–0. However, it was a different story in Australia in 1907–08 with the home side dominating the series, 4–1. Australia finished the decade with a successful defence of the Ashes in England in 1909, but the tour was not without its problems.

In the first overseas tour under the auspices of the newly established Australian Board of Control, the players refused to accept the authority of the Board-appointed vice-captain and treasurer, Peter McAlistar. But captain 'Monty' Noble was able to galvanise the talent in the team after a 10 wicket defeat in the opening Test of the series and Australia fought back to win the next two Tests. The visitors showed their resolve in drawing the final two Tests of the series (in the fifth Test at The Oval, left-hander Warren Bardsley became the first player to score centuries in both innings of a Test match). When Noble returned home with the Ashes he had the added satisfaction of having won all five tosses in the Test series.

1909

ABOVE: The first cricket team from Australia to tour over-seas was a combined Aboriginal squad in 1868 which played 47 games in England. While this photo was taken in Melbourne in 1866, many of these players were on that significant tour. The players photographed are, standing at the back: Tarpot, T.W.Willis, Mullagh. Front: King Cole (who died on tour with tuberculosis), Dick-a-Dick, Jellico, Peter, Red Cap, Harry Rose, Bullocky, Cuzens. While their skill at cricket on tour was not of a high standard, plus the problems associated with an unfamiliar climate and other obstacles,

their entertainment factor was far more impressive. The English crowds were thrilled by the player's demonstrations of boomerang throwing and other native skills.

BELOW This shot was taken in the first international cricket match ever conducted in Australia, between H.H. Stephenson's all-professional team from England and a Victorian 18. The momentous occasion was on 1st January, 1862, with England winning by an innings before a crowd of over 15,000.

The great man, W.G.Grace, and Harry Jupp, who scored England's first half-century in Test cricket in the very first Test match between Australia and England, in March 1877. Match Scores: Australia 245 (C.Bannerman 165) and 104 (A.Shaw 5 for 38, G.Ulyett 4 for 39); England 196 (H.Jupp 63, W.E.Midwinter 5 for 78) and 108 (T.Kendall 7 for 55). Australia won by 45 runs.

...they surprised all the doubters
about their ability...

RIGHT Horse drawn cabs unloading spectators outside the ground about the same time. This road is now Driver Avenue, and runs a slightly different direction.

OPPOSITE BOTTOM One of the type of steam trams which was used to carry spectators to the Sydney Cricket Ground in the early 1880s.

BELOW David Gregory's 1878 Australian team was the first full-scale tour by a team from 'down-under'. Numbering only 12, they surprised all the doubters about their ability when they defeated the MCC team at Lords. Left to right, Standing: J.M.Blackham, T.Horan, G.H.Bailey, D.W.Gregory (Captain, seated with beard), J.Conway (Manager), A.C.Bannerman, C.Bannerman, W.L.Murdoch. Front Row: F.R.Spofforth, F.Allan, W.E.Midwinter, T.W.Garrett, H.F.Boyle.

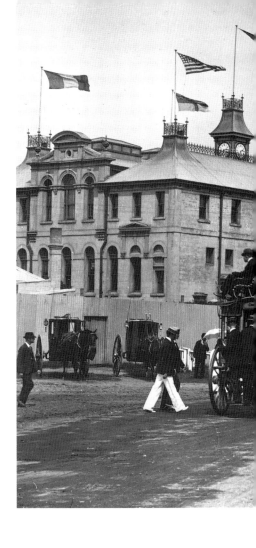

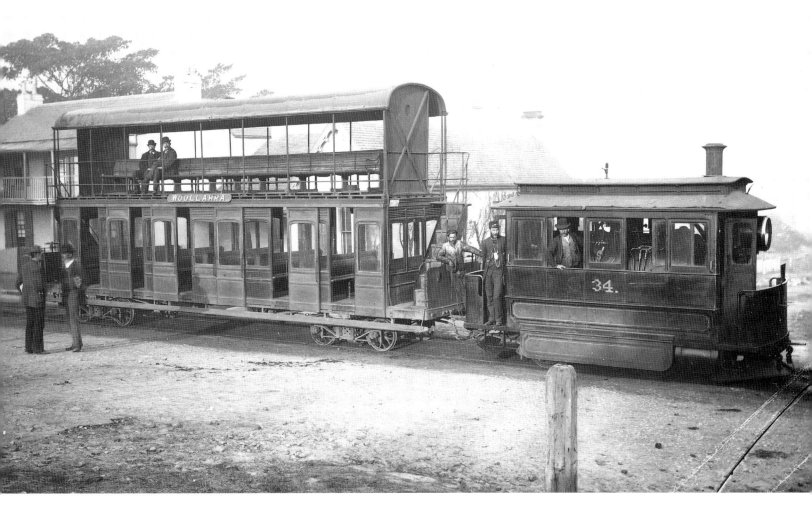

LEFT: W.L.Murdoch's 1882 team that toured England. In the only Test played the Australians had an unlikely victory, by just seven runs. This famous match and the surprising result was the catalyst for the 'Ashes', being burned because of England's demise. The scores in an amazing match were: Australia 63 (R.G.Barlow 5 for 19, E Peate 4 for 31) and 122 (H.H.Massie 55, E. Peat 4 for 40); England 101 (F.R.Spofforth 7 for 46) and 77 (F.R.Spofforth 7 for 44). Australia won by 7 runs.

BELOW W.L.Murdoch's 1882 team that toured England, was the first to defeat England at home. Left to right, Standing: T.W.Garrett, G.J.Bonnor, H.F.Boyle, H.H.Massie, G.E.Palmer, C.W.Beal (Manager), J.M.Blackham. Sitting: G.Giffen, F.R.Spofforth, T.Horan, P.S.McDonnell, W.L.Murdoch (Captain), A.C.Bannerman.

the surprising result was the catalyst for the 'Ashes' being burned

ABOVE: An early artists impression of a match played between James Lillywhite's 1887–77 English team against Victoria.

RIGHT Australia's George Bonnor, who was one of the big-hitters of the1880s. In the Fourth Test of 1884–85 at Sydney he came to the crease with Australia 6 for 119 trailing England's total of 269. When out in the middle he scored 128, while only 41 was scored by his batting partners. Match Scores: England 269 (W.Bates 64, W.Barnes 50, J.M.Read 47, A.Shrewsbury 40, G. Giffen 7 for 117) and 77 (F.R. Spofforth 5 for 30, G.E.Palmer 4 for 32); Australia 309 (G.J. Bonnor 128, A.C. Bannerman 51, S.P. Jones 40, W. Barnes 4 for 61) and 2 for 40. Australia won by 8 wickets.

...you can see a broad grin that can be seen through his beard

LEFT A younger W.G.Grace

BELOW W.G.Grace, the larger than life character, shows the style of one of his offspin deliveries, which led to many scalps.

ABOVE William Gilbert Grace, the old man who played for an astonishing 44 years, will always be synonymous with the game of cricket. He was a man ahead of his time, setting so many records, be it large scores, aggregate of runs or wickets. Here he executes one of his more orthodox hook shots during his 1891–92 tour to Australia. He played Test cricket from 1880 to 1899, playing in 22 Tests he scored 1098 runs. As he opens his shoulders there is a broad grin that can be seen through his beard.

ABOVE RIGHT Charles J.Eady, who played two Tests for Australia in 1896 and the 1901–02 series against England. His real claim to fame was when he made 566 for Break-O'-Day against Wellington at Hobart in 1902.

RIGHT 'The Demon' Spofforth's bowling partner during the 1870s and 1880s H.F. (Harry) Boyle, of Victoria. He was forever labeled 'The Very Devil', from when he captured six wickets for just three runs against the MCC at Lord's in 1878.

Brilliant images of the Sydney Cricket Ground in 1893 in a match between Victoria and New South Wales. On the left is what was later called the Brewongle Stand. In front of the stand is a tree near the fence. The middle shot has the members stand on the left and the smaller Secretary's Office on the right. The image on the right shows portion of the hill around to the Paddington end.

Images of the Sydney Cricket Ground in 1893

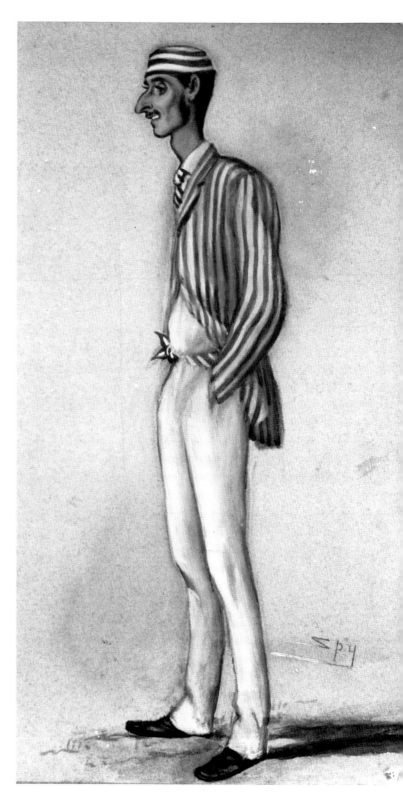

OPPOSITE PAGE TOP The 1886 Australian team in England. Standing: R.A.Thoms (umpire), J.McIlwraith, J.W.Trumble, A.H.Jarvis, W.Bruce, S.P.Jones, G.E.Palmer, F.R.Spofforth. Seated: B.J.Wardill (manager), J.M. Blackham, E.Evans, H.J.H.Scott (captain), G.J.Bonnor, T.W.Garrett, G.Giffen, F.H.Farrands (umpire). They played a total of 39 games on a tour, which was hampered greatly by rain, winning just nine, drawing 22 and losing eight. Amongst their losses were all three Tests.

OPPOSITE PAGE BOTTOM The 1893 Australians which toured England, losing the three match series by 1-0. Left to right, Standing: V.Cohen (Manager), R.W.Mcleod, W.F.Giffen, H.Trumble, J.J.Lyons, A.H.Jarvis, G.H.S.Trott. Seated: A.Coningham, W.Bruce, J.M.Blackham (Captain), G.Giffen, C.T.B.Turner. Front Row: S.E.Gregory, A.C.Bannerman, H.Graham.

ABOVE LEFT Alexander Chambers Bannerman, who was the brother of the first century maker in Test cricket, Charles Bannerman. A dour defensive player, he represented Australia in 28 Tests against England.

ABOVE RIGHT A caricature of the Australian pace bowler Frederick Robert Spofforth, dubbed 'The Demon' by his English opponents. A fast bowler, he was feared for his extreme accuracy, seam and yorkers. He captured 94 career wickets at an average of 18.41 in 18 Tests against England.

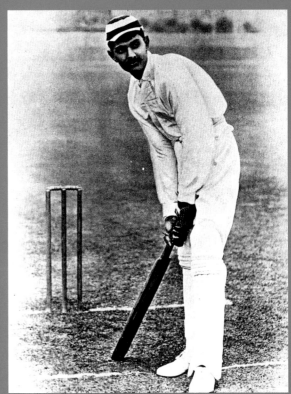

ABOVE A great shot of a full grandstand at the Sydney Cricket Ground in 1896. Notice in this image the bike track can now be seen. The track was laid that year, and was made of asphalt and was banked steeply. In the background is the Ladies and the Members pavilions. Notice in the stand in the foreground both the ladies and the gentlemen are attired in their 'Sunday best'.

RIGHT England's counterpart for Victor Trumper, the Indian born Ranjitsinhji. 'Ranji', as he was called, scored a century in his first Test against Australia (154 not out) at Old Trafford in 1896.

ABOVE Australian captain of the Golden Age, Joe Darling. He led Australia in 21 Tests, including those of the exciting 1902 series against England, which saw the first two Tests drawn, then Australia won the Third and Fourth Tests by 143 runs and 3 runs respectively. England won the final Test by 1 wicket.

ABOVE The hard-hitting Percy Stanisiaus McDonnell, who played in the 1880s. He played in 19 Tests in all from 1880-1888, captaining Australia in six against England. He scored 124 and 83 against England in the first Test match ever played at Adeiaide, in 1884–85. Match Scores: Australia 243 (P.S.McDonnell 124, J.M.Blackham 66, W.Bates 5 for 31) and 191 (P.S.McDonnell 83, G.Giffen 47, R.Peel 5 for 51); England 369 (W.Barnes 134, W.H.Scotton 82, G.Ulyett 68, G.E.Palmer 5 for 81) and 67 for 2. England won by 8 wickets.

TOP LEFT T.R.McKibbin, who took 101 wickets for the Australian Team of 1896. He played Test cricket from1894–95 to 1897–98 but his international career was cut short when Spofforth wrote to the *Sporting Times* naming him as a 'chucker'. With his action always thought to be suspect, his Test career was suddenly over.

ABOVE William Lloyd Murdoch, who captained Australia in 16 Tests against England from 1880 to 1890. He scored the very first double century in Test cricket, a score of 211 at the Oval in 1884. Previously his 153 not-out at the same venue in 1880 was the first Test century made by an Australian batsman abroad.

ABOVE The greatest left-handed batsman of his era, Clem Hill, who was from South Australia. For his state in Sheffield Shield Cricket he made 6,274 runs at 52.28, including a top score of 365 not out. In 49 Tests he scored 3,412 runs, including seven centuries. He also captained Australia against England in the 1911–12 series.

OPPOSITE PAGE Magazine cover of the day, with Australia's first great batsman, William Lloyd Murdoch and England's greatest nineteenth century cricketer, Dr William Gilbert Grace. Murdoch led the 1880, 1882 and 1884 Australian teams to England and, though, then resident in England, led the Australian side in the 1890 series there.

FAMOUS CRICKETERS
and Cricket Grounds

EDITED BY
C.W.ALCOCK.
PRICE 6D

PUBLISHED BY
HUDSON & KEARNS
83. Southwark St. London S.E.
AND
"NEWS OF THE WORLD"
9 & 10. WHITEFRIARS St. LONDON.

Border names: W.G.GRACE, G.GIFFEN, F.S.JACKSON, W.L.MURDOCH, SHREWSBURY, C.T.B.TURNER, W.W.READ, M.BLACKHAM, A.E.STODDART, G.H.STROTH, GUNN, W.BRUCE, BRIGGS, F.T.IREDALE, PEEL, ABEL, S.M.J.WOODS, BROCKWELL, BROWN, A.N.HORNBY

Photo by E. Hawkins & Co.] W. L. MURDOCH. W. G. GRACE. [Preston St., Brighton.

Photo by Simmons & Thiele. LORD'S CRICKET GROUND. Chancery Lane, E.C.

*George Giffen was the first
Australian bowler to take all
10 wickets in an innings in
first-class cricket in Australia.*

BELOW Andrew E. Stoddart, who played Test cricket for England in 16 matches, eight as captain, scored 996 runs, with a high score of 173 and an average of 35.57.

BELOW RIGHT One of Australia's most devastating hitters — Jack Lyons of South Australia. He scored 149 runs in just 95 minutes against the MCC at Lord's in 1893, reaching his century in exactly one hour.

RIGHT George Giffen, from South Australia. He was Australia's great all-rounder of the 1880s and 1890s. In the First Test of 1894–95 against England he scored 161 and 41 runs and took eight wickets. His performance in scoring 271 out of 562 and taking 9 for 96 and 7 for 70 for South Australia against Victoria at Adelaide in January of 1891 is still regarded as the greatest all-round performances in the history of first class cricket. He was the first Australian bowler to take all 10 wickets in an innings in first-class cricket in Australia. He took 10 for 66 for the Australia X1 against the Rest of Australia in 1883–84. Giffen was top order right-hand batsman and right-arm off-spin bowler.

ABOVE Australian Monty Noble on board the *Ormuz*, while in Columbo en route to England for the 1899 tour, being entertained by a snake charmer.

OPPOSITE The lunch interval in the Australians match against Sussex at New County Ground, Hove, Brighton in 1899. It was a common occurrence for the spectators to wander across the ground during the breaks for lunch and tea in those days. Although difficult to see, on the scoreboard in the middle of the image it shows Victor Trumper 300 not out and Joe Darling 45 not out and Australia 624 for 4. Trumper had batted for 380 minutes for his score, hitting 36 fours, and it beat the previous highest score by an Australian in England.

It was a common occurrence for the spectators to wander across the ground during the breaks for lunch and tea

LEFT Great off-spin bowler of the Golden Age, Hugh Trumble of Victoria. Trumble took 141 wickets at 21.78 in 32 tests and was not beaten as an Australian test Wicket-taker until Clarrie Grimmet passed him in the 1930s.

*M.A.Noble took 121 wickets,
with a career best of 7 for 17 in the
Second Test of the 1901–02 series
at Melbourne.*

OPPOSITE TOP The Australian touring side to England of 1902. Left to right, Standing: W.P.Howell, W.W.Armstrong, E.Jones, H.Trumble, Major B.Wardill (Manager), A.J.Hopkins, S.E.Gregory, C.Hill. Seated: V.T.Trumper, J.V.Saunders, J.Darling (Captain), M.A.Noble, J.J.Kelly. In Front: H.Carter, R.A.Duff. Australia won the series 2-1, with 2 matches drawn. The series was fought out by two of the great sides of early Test cricket.

ABOVE M.A.Noble, one of the true giants of the game. He debuted for Australia in the 1897–98 series against England at age 24, and before retiring in 1909, he played 42 Tests. He was a right handed batsman and scored a total of 1,997 runs, with a high score of 133 against England in the First Test of the 1903–04 series in Sydney. He also took 121 wickets, with a career best of 7 for 17 in the Second Test of the 1901–02 series at Melbourne.

Albert 'Tibby' Cotter was killed in action during the famous Beersheba Charge

ABOVE Many cricketers are remembered for the runs they amass or the wickets they capture. But only a select few are remembered for their influence on the technique of the game. Such a player was England Test bowler Bernard Bosanquet, who originated the googly. Tall and strong, he was a talented games-player, and it was on the billiards table, that he invented and developed the googly — the off-break bowled with a leg-break action. In Australia it became known as the 'Bosie'. He first bowled the googly in public at Lord's in 1900, and though, like many of his successors, he found accuracy of length elusive. His bowling played a vital part in the winning of two of his seven Test matches. In the last innings of the fourth Test at Sydney in 1903–04 he took 6-51, and at Nottingham a year later 8-107 in the first Test against Australia.

ABOVE The man who started the modern search for unorthodox bowling deliveries, B.J.T.Bosanquet. He clean bowled the great Victor Trumper with the first 'bosie' he bowled in Australia.

ABOVE Classic action shot of Victor Trumper in full flight in 1902, taken by George Beldam, the well-known English cricket photographer, at The Oval.

ABOVE RIGHT Trumper hits a tremendous square cut off a rising ball, weight right forward on the front foot, bat freely swinging.

RIGHT: A Thiele postcard of 1905 of Victor Trumper.

OPOSITE TOP LEFT AND RIGHT The Victor Trumper late cut was a thing of beauty as these two pictures demonstrate. In the first shot, Trumper waits until the ball is well past the batting crease, before hitting powerfully down on it, wrists firm. The results are seen in the second shot, with the ball speeding down to deep third man.

BELOW Victor Trumper is on 179 not out as he cuts Arnold in the second innings at the Sydney Cricket Ground in the First Test of the 1903–04 series. J.V.Saunders is the other Australian batsman. Match Scores: Australia 285 (M.A.Noble 133, E.G.Arnold 4 for 76) and 485 (V.T.Trumper 185, R.A.Duff 84, C.Hill 51, W.Rhodes 5 for 94); England 577 (R.E.Foster 287, L.C.Braund 102, J.T.Tyldesley 53) and 194 for 5 (T.Hayward 91, G.H.Hirst 60). England won by 5 wickets.

F. S. Crawford being the top scorers. Showers interrupted the play, and the second innings

H. TRUMBLE BOWLING.

twice for an aggregate of 140 runs. There was only one double-figure contribution, and

V. Trumper.	H. Trumble.	A. E. Johns.	W. Howell.	Major B. J. Wardill.	M. A. Noble.	F. Laver.	C. McLeod.
	J. J. Kelly.	Clem Hill.	J. Worrall.	J. Darling.	F. A. Iredale.	E. Jones	
				S. E. Gregory.			

THE AUSTRALIAN TEAM.

OPPOSITE TOP The 1897–98 New South Wales team. Left to right, Back Row: J.J.Kelly, V.T.Trumper, M.A.Noble, Pye, A.Conningham, Mackenzie. Seated: F.Iredale, unidentified, T.W.Garrett, W.P.Howell, H.Donnan. In Front: S.E.Gregory, H.Carter, T.R.McKibbin.

ABOVE The 1899 Australians. Standing: V.Trumper, H.Trumble, A.E.Johns, W.Howell, Major B.J.Wardill, M.A.Noble, F.Laver, C.McLeod. Seated: J.J.Kelly, C.Hill, J.Worrall, J.Darling, F.A.Iredale, E.Jones. In Front: S.E.Gregory.

OPPOSITE BOTTOM Famous portrait shot of Victor Trumper at Lord's in his famous Test cap of 1899.

Portion of the Sydney Cricket Ground hill during the Fourth Test between Australia and England, 1895. On this eventful third day Australia dismissed England twice for scores of just 65 and 72. The scoreboard in the background shows England 5 for 29 in their second innings. Match Scores: Australia 284 (H.Graham 105, A.E.Trott 85, J.Briggs 4 for 65); England 65 (G.H.S.Trott 3 for 21, C.T.B.Turner 3 for 18, G.Giffen 3 for 14) and 72 (G.Giffen 5 for 25, C.T.B.Turner 4 for 33). Australia won by an innings and 147 runs.

OPPOSITE TOP The 1905 Australians in England. Left to right, Standing:D.R.A.Gehrs, W.P.Howell, W.W.Armstrong, F.Laver, A.J.Hopkins, P.M.Newland. Seated: R.A.Duff, C.Hill, V.T.Trumper, J.Darling (Captain), M.A.Noble, C.E.McLeod, J.J.Kelly. In Front: S.E.Gregory, A.Cotter.

ABOVE With the spectators dressed in their 'finery' it is a wonderful image from the 1905 Australia v Kent match at St Lawrence Ground, Cantebury. The Australian team is in the foreground on the right hand side of the photo. In the background is a wonderful example of architecture of the times.

OPPOSITE BOTTOM From the same game as above image, but from a different angle. The Australians are relaxing on the grass watching the action in their 'boaters'. At the back on the far right facing the camera is Frank Iredale (with the bushy moustache). Tibby Cotter is in the foreground leaning back and Joe Darling, the captain, is leaning foreward with his hat back off his forehead with a smaller moustache.

LEFT The Victorian internationals at the Melbourne Cricket Ground in 1905 for a game against New South Wales. They are: C.McLeod (far left), H.Trumble (second from left), B.Ransford (middle), W.Armstrong (far right) and G.Hazelett (foreground on right).

BELOW W.W.Armstrong, who played for Australia from1901 to 1921, in 50 Tests, scored 2863 runs at an average of 38.68, took 87 wickets at 33.59. The 'big ship' led arguably the greatest Australian side of all-time in the 1921 series in England. They won the five Test series 3–0. Of 38 matches played on tour, they won 22, drew 14, with the only 2 losses coming at the end of the tour when interest waned after their substantial bonus of 300 pounds per player was assured.

OPPOSITE TOP LEFT: An intriguing shot of legendary Australian cricketer Syd Gregory who, when batting preferred slatted pads, cummerbund, disdained gloves. He also wore a curious square-brimmed hat.

OPPOSITE BOTTOM LEFT AND RIGHT Sydney Edward Gregory made his first tour to England in 1890 at the age of 20 and played in 58 Test matches for a further 22 years, scoring 2282 runs. He made eight tours of England, captaining his country in six Tests in 1912 at the age of 42, after 'the big six'(Carter, Trumper, Armstrong, Hill, Cotter and Ransford) pulled out after a disagreement on tour conditions with the Australian Board of Control.

Bert Oldfield ... built up a reputation for never appealing when the batsman was not out.

THREE FAMOUS AUSTRALIAN WICKET-KEEPERS: (Top left) Hanson Carter, who played 28 Tests from 1907–1922 took 44 catches and 21 stumpings, demonstrates his stumping technique. A Yorkshire-born undertaker, who played for New South Wales and Australia from 1907 until 1921, he took pace men and spinners with equal ability. (Top right) Barry Jarman, who played 19 Tests for Australia from 1959–1969 took 50 catches and 4 stumpings. The Adelaide sports goods store proprietor took a catch in a Test at Melbourne which ranks with one of Carter's best. (Opposite left) Bert Oldfield, who played 54 Tests from 1920–1937 took 78 catches and 52 stumpings. Neat and craftsmanlike in all his work, he built up a reputation for never appealing when the batsman wasn't out. When he appealed umpires took notice.

ABOVE RIGHT The Charles George Macartney stance in 1909. He played 35 Tests for Australia from 1907–1926, was top order right hand batsman, who scored 2131 runs, with a career best of 170 at an average of 41.78 and took 45 wickets at 27.55, with a best of 7 for 58. He is one of the lesser known legends, who played at the highest level for 19 years.

RIGHT Leslie Oswald Sheridan Poidevin, debuted for New South Wales in the 1895–96 season, and thereafter spent many years playing in England. He was also the Australian Board of Control's representative in England during that time. His legacy to cricket can still be seen in the playing of the Poidevin Gray Shield, which originated in the 1920s in Sydney. A man of many talents, he also represented Australia in Davis Cup tennis, and graduated from the University of Edinburgh as a doctor of medicine.

The Australian 1912 team to tour England to play a triangular series against South Africa and England. Considered one of the weak-
est teams to leave our shores, they defeated South Africa 2–0, with one drawn but lost to the tournament champions England 1–0, with
two draws. Weakened by the absence of 'the big six', captain Syd Gregory was on his eighth and final tour to England. Left to right:
Back Row: G.S.Crouch (Manager), R.B.Minnett, E.Hume (Visitor), C.Kelleway, E.R.Mayne, S.H.Emery, D.Smith, W.J.Whitty,
H.Webster, C.B.Hazlitt. Front Row: W.Bardsley, J.W.McLaren, T.J.Matthews, S.E.Gregory (Captain), C.B.Jennings, C.G.McCartney

1910 – 1929

2

1910

THE PERIOD FROM 1910–29 WAS DOMINATED BY THE ADVENT OF WORLD WAR I in 1914, which ended international cricket competition for five years, and then by the post-war resurgence of the game in the 1920s. Australia hosted South Africa (1910–11) and England (1911–12) in consecutive summers before meeting with these nations in a triangular Test series in England in 1912. England and Australia would not meet again until J.W.H.T.Douglas' team would travel to Australia's shores in 1920–21.

In 1910-11 South Africa became the first non-English team to play a Test series in Australia. Australia scored 528 in the first innings of the opening Test (132 by Warren Bardsley and a magnificent 191 by Clem Hill) and bowled the South Africans out for 174 and 240 (Albert 'Tibby' Cotter and Bill Whitty took eight wickets each.) Australia ultimately won the five-Test series 4-1, but the South Africans recorded their first Test win against Australia on a placid Adelaide wicket in the fourth Test of the series.

the declaration of war in the summer of 1914 plunged Europe, Australia and ultimately the United States into the Great War

Australia's battle to retain the Ashes won in England in 1909 was fought on and off the field in the summer of 1911–12. Captained by Clem Hill, Australia won the first Test by 146 runs after 'googly' bowler Dr Herbert 'Ranji' Hordern took 12/175. However, Australia buckled under the attack of Frank Foster and lost the next two Tests of the series. Before the fourth Test, Clem Hill came to blows with Australian selector Peter McAlister after six prominent players — including Hill, Warwick Armstrong, Victor Trumper and 'Tibby' Cotter—opposed the Board-appointed manager (George Crouch) for the coming tour of England. In the end, the Board had their way and the dissenting players were left out of the 1912 Ashes tour. Not surprisingly, Australia lost the final two Tests of the series — and the Ashes — and Hill's international career was over.

Syd Gregory, aged 42, was recalled to the Test arena to lead Australia to England for a triangular Test series against England and South Africa. 'Little Tich' Gregory, who made his Test debut back in 1890, was seen as a 'Board' man and received little co-operation from his players on the troubled tour. Manager George Crouch ignored a telegram from the Board suggesting the tour be called off because of poor player behaviour but there were some memorable performances on the field. Although Australia did not win a Test

Yes, I would like to subscribe to *Vogue Living*:

Me Gift
☐ ☐ 1 year (6 issues) Australia $39.95
☐ ☐ 2 years (12 issues) Australia $74.95
☐ ☐ 1 year (6 issues) NZ AU$70.00
☐ ☐ 1 year (6 issues) Overseas AU$90.00

MY DETAILS:

Mr/Mrs/Miss/Ms (Full name): _____

Address: _____ Suburb: _____ State: _____ Postcode: _____

Daytime phone: _____ Email: _____

GIFT RECIPIENT DETAILS:

Mr/Mrs/Miss/Ms (Full name): _____

Address: _____ Suburb: _____ State: _____ Postcode: _____

Daytime phone: _____ Email: _____

Please send a gift announcement card to: ☐ Me ☐ Gift recipient

PAYMENT DETAILS:

Please find enclosed my cheque/money order for $_____ payable to FPC Magazines

Or charge my: ☐ Visa ☐ MasterCard ☐ Diners Club ☐ Amex

Cardholder's name: _____

Card number:

☐☐☐☐ ☐☐☐☐ ☐☐☐☐ ☐☐☐☐

Cardholder's signature: _____ Expiry date: ___/___

TO ORDER:

📞 **1300 656 933**
Overseas dial +61 2 8296 5424

🖱 suscribenow.com.au/
vogueliving/2801

Send original or copy of this
coupon (no stamp required) to:
✉ **News Magazines,
Reply Paid 1224,
Queen Victoria Building
NSW 1229**

2801

Subscribe &
save up to
21%

Pay only $39.95 for a one year subscription and be inspired with each issue.

Vogue Living is dedicated to showing you the world's most beautiful interiors.

Each issue is a visual feast, layered with information on the latest in international design trends, fabrics, furniture, art, decorating and architecture.

USA and Canada in June 1913, playing five matches (four in Philadelphia and one in Toronto), but the declaration of war in the summer of 1914 plunged Europe, Australia and ultimately the United States into the Great War. The Australian Board of Control had selected a team to tour South Africa in 1914–15 under the captaincy of Warwick Armstrong but the tour was abandoned in August 1914 after the declaration of war. However, the Board pressed ahead with the Sheffield Shield season in the first Australian summer of the war. However, the respective State selectors found it difficult to pick teams that could train with any enthusiasm or arouse public interest in attending cricket matches. World War I (1914–18) stopped domestic and international cricket competition in their tracks.

'Enlist in the Sportsmen's Thousand: Show the Enemy What Australian Sporting Men Can Do.'

A series of 'Patriotic Matches' were also played during the summer of 1914–15 as Australian troops prepared to sail for Egypt on their way to a far-off corner of the globe called Gallipoli. One recruitment poster of the day asked: 'Enlist in the Sportsmen's Thousand: Show the Enemy What Australian Sporting Men Can Do.' 'Tibby' Cotter, the Australian fast bowler and Test veteran, took up the challenge but was killed in the charge of the Light Horse at Beersheba in 1917. In the first year of the war, as thousands of Australian and New Zealand troops dug in at the Dardanelles, the Australian sporting public was shocked by the premature death of Victor Trumper. The former star NSW and Australian batsman had been in declining health after developing Bright's disease and passed away on 28 June 1915, aged just 37.

In January 1919, with the Great War over, a cricket team was formed by Australian Imperial Forces (AIF) still stationed in England. Herb Collins led the team in 28 first class matches during the first summer of peace; playing in England and South Africa before retuning to Australia in Christmas 1919. The AIF team played two unofficial 'Tests' in South Africa, with Collins scoring 235 and taking 5/52 in the first of these matches.

England was invited to tour Australia in the summer of 1919–20 but the request was declined by the MCC because it was seen as too soon after the end of the war.

The English team that toured Australia in 1911/12. Third from left in the centre row is their captain, Sir Pelham 'Plum' Warner. He had to undergo a serious operation in Melbourne, and handed the captaincy over to J.W.H.T.Douglas. England ended up winning the series 4-1, after losing the First Test. Left to right, Back Row: S.P.Kinneir, E.J.Smith, F.E.Woolley, S.F.Barnes, J.Iremonger, R.C.Campbell (visitor), J.Vine, H.Strudwick; Seated: W.Rhodes, J.W.H.T.Douglas, P.F.Warner (Captain), F.R.Foster, T.Pawley (Manager), J.B.Hobbs, G.Gunn; Front: J.W.Hearne, J.W.Hitch; Inset: C.P.Mead.

1929

1910

Instead, the first post-war Ashes series did not get under way until December 1920 — but only after the England team was quarantined following an outbreak of typhoid on the trip to Australia. The home team won the first Test by 377 runs after second innings centuries by Collins (104) and captain Warwick Armstrong (158). For the first time in Ashes history, Australia completed a clean sweep in the series, 5–0, against the English team. Australia won each Test handsomely against Johnny Douglas' team — by 377 runs, an innings and 91 runs, 119 runs, eight wickets and nine wickets. Australian bowler Arthur Mailey took a record 36 wickets in the Ashes series.

The 1921 Australian tour of England started in sensational fashion when Arthur Mailey captured all ten second-innings wickets in the match against Gloucester. Warwick Armstrong's Australian team retained the Ashes with a 3–nil Test series victory; the giant batsman taking his unbeaten record as captain to eight wins from ten Ashes Tests. Stricken with malaria and troubled by leg problems on the long journey home, Armstrong's giant frame finally gave out and Herb Collins took over as captain on the six-match, three-Test tour of South Africa. At Johannesburg in the second Test of the series, Jack Gregory scored the fastest century in Test history — 100 in just 70 minutes off 67 balls — and the manner in which it was scored even overshadowed Herb Collins' 203. Australia secured the series with a 10 wicket victory in Cape Town in the third Test.

in the late 1920s, a teenage batsman from Bowral in Country NSW came to prominence and would eclipse every record in the game

It was another three years of domestic Shield cricket before England returned to Australia in search of the Ashes in 1924–25. The tour by Arthur Gilligan's English team was widely anticipated by Australian crowds who had flocked to Shield matches during the previous summer. Bill Ponsford, who scored a first class record 429 in Victoria's incredible first innings score of 1059 in February 1923, scored a century on debut in Australia's first Test victory at the SCG. Ponsford posted another ton in Australia's record score of 600 runs in the first innings of the second Test win in Melbourne before a narrow 11 run victory in the third Test of the series secured the Ashes. England ended an eleven-Test losing streak with a belated victory in the fourth Test of the series before the bowling of Clarrie Grimmett (11/82 for the match) curtailed any chance of England saving face in Australia's 307 run victory in the fifth Test in Sydney.

Herb 'Lucky' Collins did not live up to his name when he led Australia to England to defend the Ashes in 1926. A passionate gambler, Collins' luck ran out in a series marred by poor weather. Only 32 runs were scored in the first Test at Nottingham before the match was abandoned. A magnificent 193 by Bardsley in the first innings and Charles Macartney's 133 not out in the second innings saved the second Test. Not even centuries by Bill Woodfull and Macartney in both the third and fourth Tests of the series could force a result. In the deciding Test at the Oval, England selectors changed captains (Percy

Chapman for Arthur Carr) but Australia led after the first innings. Centuries by Jack Hobbs and Herb Sutcliffe set up a 415 lead for England before bowlers Harold Larwood (3/14) and Wilfred Rhodes (4/44) won the Ashes with a day to play. 37 year-old Herb Collins did not play in another Test match.

The years leading up to the 1928–29 Ashes series were dominated by the deeds of Bill Ponsford (352 in Victoria's total of 1107 in December 1926 and a world record 437 against Queensland in February 1928). But in the late 1920s, a teenage batsman from Bowral in Country NSW came to prominence and would eclipse every record in the game. Donald George Bradman was born at Cootamundra (NSW) on 27 August 1908. Legend says that the youngster developed his hand-eye co-ordination by repeatedly bouncing a golf ball off a corrugated water-tank using a cricket stump as a bat. The feats of the then 17 year-old in the local Bowral 'A Grade' competition earned him an invitation by the NSW Cricket Association to attend training in Sydney in October 1926. Bradman scored 110 on debut for the St George Club that summer and then posted 118 on debut for NSW against South Australia the following year.

the Ashes result may have been somewhat different had England held on to its catches

Bradman made his Test debut against Percy Chapman's England team in Brisbane in the first Test of the 1928–29 Ashes series. Batting at number seven, the wiry right-hander made scores of just 18 and 1 in Australia's mammoth 675 run defeat and was dropped to twelfth man for the second Test in Sydney. England won the match by eight wickets and Bradman was reinstated for the vital third Test of the series. The 20 year-old budding champion was one of six players to score a century in the match (Kippax 100, captain Jack Ryder 112, Woodfull 107 and Bradman 112 for Australia and Hammond 200, and Sutcliffe 135 for England) but the visitors won the high-scoring match (with almost 1500 runs scored) in Melbourne by 3 wickets. England won the fourth Test by only 12 runs to take a 4-0 lead in the series before Australia — highlighted by centuries to Woodfull and Bradman — won the final Test of the series. Jack Ryder, already pushing 40 years of age, would not be selected on the Ashes tour of England in 1930 — the Australian Board of Control would pursue a 'youth' policy and in young Don Bradman, they held the future of international cricket.

After a period of enormous stock-market upheaval, the share prices on the New York Stock Exchange in Wall Street collapsed on 'Black Tuesday' — 29 October 1929. The 'Great Crash of '29' set off a chain reaction of events that ultimately plunged the western industrialised nations — including Australia — into economic Depression during the early 1930s. But for the time being, the nation's eyes were diverted away from the human tragedy that was unfolding across the world.

In the first week of 1930, Don Bradman scored 452 not out for NSW in the Shield match against Queensland and may have even surpassed 500 runs had captain Alan Kippax not declared. Having started the new decade by beating Bill Ponsford's batting record, Bradman — 'The Don' — would make the 1930s his own.

1929

Scoreboard:
S.A. 1ST INN 575
2ND
NSW INN 279
2ND
C.HILL 365
BOWLERS WKTS RUNS
WICKETS 10
TOTAL 575

NOBLE
MARSH 5 57
HOWELL 2 181
TRUMPER 109 BOWLER
HOPKINS 3 67
GREGORY 116
12

BATSMEN OUT RUNS
LEAK
MACK
C.CIFFIN
JARVIS 71
REEDMAN
STUART
MATHEWS 12
JARVIS
WALKLEY
TRAVERS 5

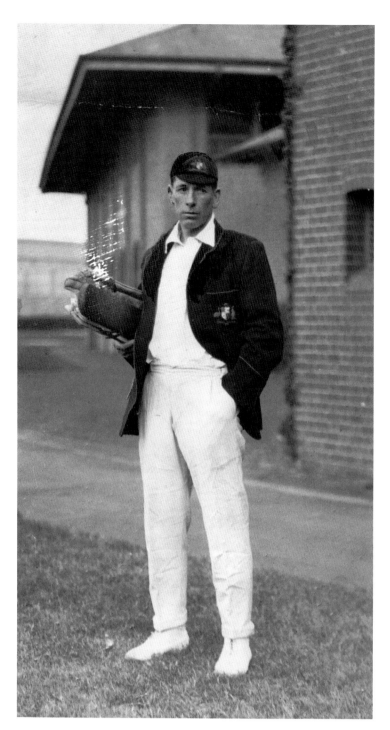

ABOVE Clem Hill and the scoreboard after he scored a prodigious 365 for South Australia against New South Wales in the 1900–01 season in Adelaide. He batted for 8 hours 35 mins and hit 35 fours and an eight!

RIGHT Clem Hill, another one of Australia's great batsman from the 'Golden Age' of cricket. His Test career spanned the years 1896 to 1912, he played in 49 Tests, scored 3412 runs at 39.21, with a high score of 191. He was a four time English tourist (1896, 1899, 1902, 1905), captained his country in Ten Tests and died an unfortunate death from terrible injuries suffered from a fall on a Melbourne tram in 1945.

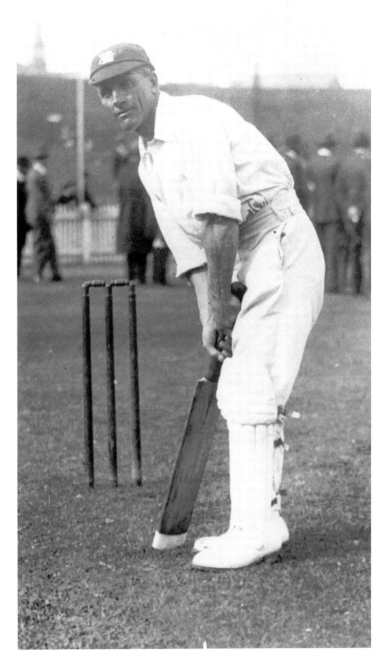

ABOVE LEFT AND RIGHT Englishman Herbert Strudwick, a wicketkeeper, who played 28 Tests from 1909 to 1926, took 60 catches and 12 stumpings. His run-getting was meagre to say the least, scoring a bare 230 runs at 7.93.

OPPOSITE BOTTOM LEFT AND RIGHT Frank Woolley, who played 64 Tests for England from 1909 to 1934, playing until he was 46 years of age. His record was: 3283 runs at 36.07, with a high score of 154 in his five Test centuries, and he took 83 wickets at 33.91.

LEFT One of England's truly great fast bowlers, Sydney F.Barnes. He played 27 Tests for England from 1901 to 1914 and took 189 wickets at 16.43, including 5 wickets in an innings 24 times, with a best return of 9 for 103.

ABOVE Raymond 'Mick' Bardsley, brother of Warren, played 11 games for New South Wales during the 1920s, and toured Malaysia with an Australian X1 during 1927.

RIGHT Warren Bardsley, played 41 Test from 1909-1926 for 2469 runs at 40.47, scored six centuries with a top score of 193 not out. Scored most of his runs as an opener, he was a non-smoker, tea-totaller and a vegetarian.

OPPOSITE top An unheralded New South Wales team of 1911, that toured the country areas of North Queensland.

OPPOSITE BOTTOM Preparing for the slaughter, Australian team about to take position for England's first innings of 589 in the Fourth Test of 1911–12 at Melbourne. In this innings J.B.Hobbs and W.Rhodes compiled the record first innings stand of 323. Players (left to right) are: Clem Hill (captain), Vernon Ransford, Charles Kelleway, Herbert Hordern, Warwick Armstrong, Albert Cotter, Hanson Carter, Victor Trumper, Roy Minnett, James Matthews and Warren Bardsley.

LEFT Australia's first googly bowler — Herbert Vivian Hordern of New South Wales. A Sydney dentist, Hordern took 46 wickets in seven Tests against South Africa and England in 1910–11 and 1911–12. While much better Australian spin bowlers followed, including Mailey, Grimmett, O'Reilly, Benaud and Warne, his claim to fame is he pioneered the googly.

OPPOSITE TOP Victor Trumper, stepping back to cut England shock leg-theory bowler F.R.Foster to the vacant off boundary during the Fourth Test at Melbourne of 1911–12. This was Trumper's second-last Test appearance. England bowler Leonard Braund once said: 'I put the ball where I wanted to, and then Vic put it where he wanted to.'

OPPOSITE BOTTOM Trumper facing F.R.Foster's lifting leg-theory in the same match as above. He was bowled by Foster for 17 in this innings. In the First Test at Sydney he scored a century against this attack, from which bodyline bowling evolved.

Four extremely rare images from the Third Test of the 1912 series between Australia and England at The Oval.

ABOVE In this shot Whitty (Australia) is brought to his knees with a ball from Woolley.

BELOW Charlie Kelleway, who top scored for Australia with 43, is out leg before wicket to Woolley in the first innings. Woolley took 10 wickets in this match.

ABOVE Bardsley (Australia) is clean bowled by Barnes. Note the middle stump out.

BELOW Minnett (Australia) being caught by Rhodes, the famous Yorkshire player. The scores in this match were: England 245 (J.B.Hobbs 66, F.E.Woolley 62, W.Rhodes 49, R.B.Minnett 4 for 34, W.J.Whitty 4 for 69) and 175 (C.B.Fry 79, G.R.Hazlitt 7 for 25); Australia 111 (C.Kelleway 43, F.E.Woolley 5 for 29, S.F.Barnes 5 for 30) and 65 (F.E.Woolley 5 for 20, H.Dean 4 for 19). England won by 244 runs.

LEFT Cecil Parkin, who played 10 Tests for England from 1920-24, was a right hand bowler who bowled a mixture of seam and spin, took 32 wickets, including a career best of 5 for 38 in 1921 in England.

BELOW Charlie Kelleway played for Australia in 26 Tests from 1910–11 to 1928–29. A very good all-rounder, he scored 1422 runs at an average of 37.42, including three centuries with a high score of 147 and he also took 52 wickets at 32.36. He was a captain in the Australian army in World War 1 and was selected to captain the AIF cricket team at war's end. His last Test in 1928–29 was Don Bradman's debut.

OPPOSTIE TOP Fourth Test of the 1921 series at Old Trafford with C.H.Parkin bowling for England. He took five wickets in this game to help dismiss Australia cheaply in their first innings. The match scores were: England 362 for 4 dec (A.C.Russell 101, E.Tyldesley 78, C.P.Mead 47, P.G.H.Fender 44, F.E.Woolley 41) and 44 for 1; Australia 175 (H.L.Collins 40, C.H.Parkin 5 for 38). Match drawn.

OPPOSITE BOTTOM Cecil Parkin sends one down in the third Test match of the 1921 series at Headingly, Leeds. After Australia had won the first two Tests in the series, by 10 wickets at Trent Bridge and 8 wickets at Lord's, they made it three in a row with a comprehensive winin this match also. Match score: Australia 407 (C.G.Macartney 115, W.W.Armstrong 77, C.E.Pellew 52, J.M.Taylor 50, C.H.Parkin 4 for 106) and 273 doe 7 dec (T.J.E.Andrews 92, H.Carter 47); England 259 (J.W.H.T.Douglas 75, L.H.Tennyson 63, G.Brown 57, E.A.McDonald 4 for 105) and 202 (G.Brown 46). Australia won by 219 runs.

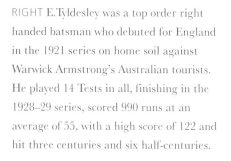

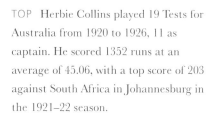

TOP Herbie Collins played 19 Tests for Australia from 1920 to 1926, 11 as captain. He scored 1352 runs at an average of 45.06, with a top score of 203 against South Africa in Johannesburg in the 1921–22 season.

.

ABOVE RIGHT Collins, a bookie and a man who liked a wager, at age 51 married the 24-year-old daughter of a race club steward.

RIGHT E. Tyldesley was a top order right handed batsman who debuted for England in the 1921 series on home soil against Warwick Armstrong's Australian tourists. He played 14 Tests in all, finishing in the 1928–29 series, scored 990 runs at an average of 55, with a high score of 122 and hit three centuries and six half-centuries.

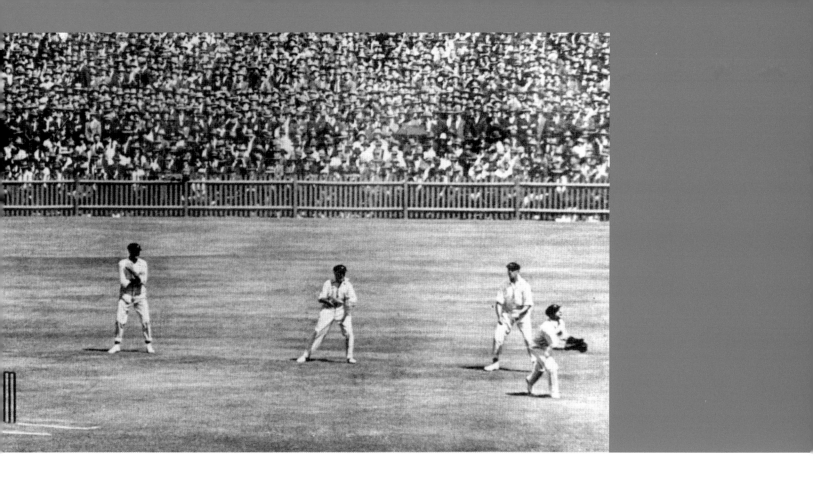

ABOVE The great Englishman J.B.Hobbs is caught by the keeper Oldfield down the leg side off Gregory at the Sydney Cricket Ground. The win by Australia in this Test gave them the series by a 4–1 margin. England were mesmorised in both innings by the 33 year-old leg-spinner Clarrie Grimmett, who captured 11 wickets in the match. Match scores: Australia 295 (W.H.Ponsford 80, A.F.Kippax 42, M.W.Tate 4 for 92, R.Kilner 4 for 97) and 325 (T.J.E.Andrews 80, C.Kelleway 73, W.A.S.Oldfield 65, M.W.Tate 5 for 115); England 167 (F.E.Woolley 47, C.V.Grimmett 5 for 45) and 146 (C.V.Grimmett 6 for 37). Australia won by 307 runs.

RIGHT: Herbie Collins, captain of Australia's 1926 Test team (in foreground) with J.M.Gregory and C.V.Grimmett (in mufti) watch as Australia plays Minor Counties at Holyport, near Maidenhead.

ABOVE This photo was taken by the Bowral Cricket Club's ground in Glebe Park, Bowral, around 1925. Don Bradman's father is the umpire at square leg. The ground has since been re-named, and is now called Bradman Oval.

LEFT Don Bradman at 16 years of age in Bowral.

Just a couple of young brothers getting their photo taken in the back yard in their 'Sunday best', see Don Bradman with his brother Vic.

The feats of the then 17 year-old in the local Bowral 'A Grade' competition earned him an invitation by the NSW Cricket Association to attend training in Sydney

LEFT The New South Welshman, Alan Kippax, who until Michael Bevan passed his runs tally, was the leading run-scorer of all-time for the state. He scored 6096 runs at an average of 70.88, with a high score of 315 against Queensland in 1927-28. In the next season he shared a world record tenth wicket stand of 307 with J.E.H.Hooker. For Australia he played in 22 Tests, from 1924-1934, scoring 1192 runs at an average of 36.12, and a high score of 146 against the Wests Indies in 1930.

OPPOSITE TOP At Johannesburg against South Africa in 1921–22 Gregory scored 100 in 70 minutes, which is still the fastest century compiled in actual time. The 67 balls faced in that innings is second behind the great West Indian Vivian Richard, who bettered it in 1985–86 against England when he scored a century in 56 balls.

OPPOSITE BOTTOM Australian all-rounder Jack Gregory, who scored 1146 runs at 36.96 in 24 Tests from 1920–1929, executes an off-drive, with Herbert Strudwick the wicket-keeper.

BELOW Jack Gregory, the right-arm fast bowler, took 85 Test wickets at an average of 31.15, with best figures of 7 for 69 against England in the second Test of the 1920–21 Ashes series.

ABOVE A great shot of the 1921 Australian Cricket and Rugby League tourists in England. The 'Big Ship' appears larger than any of the footballers!

LEFT Warwick Armstrong, or the 'Big Ship' as he was affectionately named, was a great player for Australia both as a huge hard-driving batsman and impeccably accurate slow leg and top spin bowler. Under Armstrong, Australia won eight tests in succession against England and drew two.

OPPOSITE Warwick Armstrong warms up at Lord's for the camera in 1905. On the right he is shown batting in the Fifth Test at the Oval in 1921. Armstrong scored 2,863 runs, took 87 wickets and held 44 catches in 50 Tests.

Warwick Armstrong was a huge hard-driving batsman and impeccably accurate slow leg and top spin bowler

Arthur Mailey, the most dangerous Australian bowler of the immediate post-war period.

ABOVE LEFT The most dangerous Australian bowler of the immediate post-war period, Arthur Mailey, who in 1920–21 took 36 wickets in a Test series, including nine in an innings in the fourth Test (the tenth was dropped off his bowling), which Australia won by 8 wickets. He was also a well-known journalist and artist of witty caricatures, which were published in several books.

ABOVE RIGHT Warren Bardsley, one of the greatest left-handed batsman Australia has produced. A stylish player with an upright stance and straight bat, his strength was off the front foot.

ABOVE LEFT Clarrie Grimmett, who was born in New Zealand, played 37 Tests for Australia from 1924–1936, took 216 wickets at 24.21, with a best of 7–40 against South Africa in 1936. A signwriter by trade he didn't debut until he was 33 and, when he departed the Test scene, he was 45.

TOP RIGHT E.A.McDonald was one of Australia's main strike weapons of Armstrong's 1920–21 teams. A fast bowler, he is seen here in the opening match of the 1921 Australian tour of England. The high, beautifully co-ordinated action brought him 8 for 41 this day against Leicester. His Test career yielded 43 wickets from just 11 matches, from 1920–1922. His life was cut short at just 39, when involved in a motor accident.

BOTTOM RIGHT Herbert Sutcliffe, one half of the 'Hobbs, Sutcliffe', probably the greatest English opening combinations of all-time.

OPPOSITE LEFT A get together of some of Australia's great cricketers at the Melbourne Cricket Ground in the 1920s. Left to right: Vernon Ransford, Clem Hill, M.A.Noble, Hugh Trumble, Jack Gregory, Joe Darling, unidentified, Warwick Armstrong.

BOTTOM LEFT The 1921 Australia team in England. Left to right, Standing: W.Bardsley, J.Ryder, H.S.T.L.Hendry, J.M.Gregory, E.R.Mayne, T.J.Andrews, S.Smith (Manager). Seated: A.A.Mailey, E.A.McDonald, H.L.Collins, W.W.Armstrong (Captain), C.G.Macartney, H.Carter, J.M.Taylor. In Front: C.E.Pellew, W.A.Oldfield.

LEFT AND RIGHT Early photos of J.W.H.T.Douglas, the England captain of the 1920-21 side. He captained his country in 18 Tests in all, and played Test cricket from 1911–1925. An all-rounder he scored 962 runs at an average of 29.15 and took 45 wickets at 33.02. Nicknamed 'Johnny Won't Hit Today', in reference to his penchant for defensive play, he was also a middleweight boxer who fought at the 1908 Olympic Games in London. He died a tragic death at age 48, when he tries unsuccessfully to save his drowning father after two ships had collided in rough seas off Denmark.

Bert Ironmonger spun the ball off the top of his fingers, after they were partially lost in a buzz-saw accident

ABOVE Famous Australian left-arm bowler Bert Ironmonger, who spun the ball off the top of his fingers, after they were partially lost in a buzz-saw accident when just a child. He made his Test debut at 45 (fourth oldest in Test history) and took a total of 74 Test wickets in just 14 Tests, with his best figures against South Africa of 11–24. Played his last Test at age 50.

RIGHT Hunter 'Stork' Hendry, played 11 Tests for Australia, from 1921 to 1929, scoring 335 at 20.93 and taking 16 wickets.

ABOVE 'Stork' Hendry's dismissal, leg before wicket to Harold
Larwood in the first Test at Brisbane in 1928–29. On the
Saturday he had been given not out caught behind off Maurice
Tate's bowling, much to the disappointment of the Englishmen.
Hendry said that Jack Hobbs called out to Tate, loud enough
for Hendry and the umpire to hear, that he had been unlucky.
On Monday morning (Sunday was a rest day), Hendry tried to
glance a ball which he insisted was 15cm outside his leg stump,
was hit on the left leg and given out. Hendy believed that some
of the English players complained to the umpire after the previous day's play, putting him under pressure to accept the next
appeal. The picture shows the umpire looking sheepish about
his decision, Hendry looking with amazement at the position of
his left leg, and Larwood apparently counting his blessings.
The other batsman is Jack Ryder and the match was Don
Bradman's first Test.

RIGHT 'Patsy' Hendren, the great Middlesex and England
batsman, at the Sydney Cricket Ground No.2. during the
1920s. His career spanned from 1920–1935, playing in 51 Tests
he scored 3525 at an average of 47.63, with a high score of 205
not out against the Wests Indies in 1930. A real character of
the game he could often be relied upon to lighten up proceedings on the field if the play was dull, with some comic antics.

OPPOSITE TOP Australia's First Test team of 1928 in Brisbane, which was Bradman's first Test match. Left to right, Back Row: A.F.Kippax, R.Oxenham, W.H.Ponsford. Middle Row: Umpire Hele, C.Kelleway, J.M.Gregory, H.S.T.L.Hendry, H.Ironmonger, Umpire Elder. Sitting: W.A.Oldfield, C.V.Grimmett, J.Ryder (Captain), D.G.Bradman, W.M.Woodfull. Match Scores: England 521 (E.H.Hendren 169, H.Larwood 70, A.P.F.Chapman 50, J.B.Hobbs 49, W.R.Hammond 44) and 432 for 8 dec (C.P.Mead 73, D.R.Jardine 65, E.H.Hendren 45, C.V.Grimmett 6 for 131); Australia 122 (H.Larwood 6 for 32) and 66 (J.C.White 4 for 7). England won by 675 runs.

OPPOSITE BOTTOM The Australian team for the Second Test match in Sydney on December 14-20, 1928. This Test was significant in that it was the only time the great Don Bradman was named twelfth man for Australia. Left to right, Standing: W.M.Woodfull, W.H.Ponsford, H.Ironmonger, D.J.Blackie, O.E.Nothling, H.S.T.L.Hendry. Seated: V.Y.Richardson, C.V.Grimmett, J.Ryder (Captain), D.G.Bradman, W.A.Oldfield, A.F.Kippax. Match scores were: Australia 253 (W.M.Woodfull 68, W.A.S.Oldfield 41, G.Geary 5 for 35) and 397 (H.S.T.L.Hendry 112, W.M.Woodfull 111, J.Ryder 79, O.E.Nothling 44, M.W.Tate 4 for 99); England 636 (W.R.Hammond 251, E.H.Hendren 74, G.Geary 66, H.Larwood 43, J.B.Hobbs 40, D.D.Blackie 4 for 148 and 16 for 2. England won by 8 wickets. Hammond's innings of 251 was the first double-century ever scored by an Englishman against Australia.

ABOVE The New South Wales cricket team in December, 1927, about to embark on their southern tour. Left to right, Back Row: N.Phillips, F.Jordan, A.Scanes, S.Everett, T.J.E.Andrews, D.G.Bradman, A.Jackson, W.A.Oldfield.Front Row: G.Morgan, A.F.Kippax (captain), Dr.F.V.McAdam (manager), R.McNamee, A.Mailey.

ABOVE LEFT The 'Grand Old Man' and 'Surrey Master', J.B. (later Sir Jack) Hobbs pictured beside a portrait of Dr.W.G.Grace. Hobbs scored 244 centuries, 197 of them in first-class cricket. Grace scored 217 centuries, 117 in first-class matches.

LEFT BOTTOM Victor Richardson in October of 1928. The grandfather of the famous Chappell brothers, Vic was a great all-round sportsman. Aside from playing in 19 Tests for Australia from 1924 to 1936, he also was a very good baseball player, golfer, tennis player, swimmer and was adept at lacrosse. His Test cricket career yielded 706 runs at 23.53, with a top score of 138 (his only century). He was also known for his agile fielding, which wasn't surprising considering his all-round sporting athletisism.

ABOVE Alan Fairfax at the Sydney Cricket Ground No.2. With his emergence at the same time as Don Bradman and Archie Jackson, his promise was lost to Australia, when he migrated to England in 1932 to pursue a professional cricket career with Accrington and later an indoor cricket school.

ABOVE Arthur Mailey's 'Bohemians'. Left to right, Back Row: F.Merchant, C.Nicholls, E.L.Waddy, J.Ellis, J.C.Bancks, C.Wright, T.J.E.Andrews, C.Spencer. Front Row: N.Cameron, A.Mailey, Don Bradman. This shot was taken at Dudauman, NSW in 1928. The 'Bohemians' were a team selected by Arthur Mailey, who toured country centres in New South Wales during the 1920s.

LEFT England's 1926 captain, A.P.F.Chapman, who played in 26 Tests from 19024 to 1931, scoring 925 at an average 28.9, with a high score of 121, and captained his country in 17 Tests.

The grandfather of the famous Chappell brothers, Victor Rchardson was a great all-round sportsman.

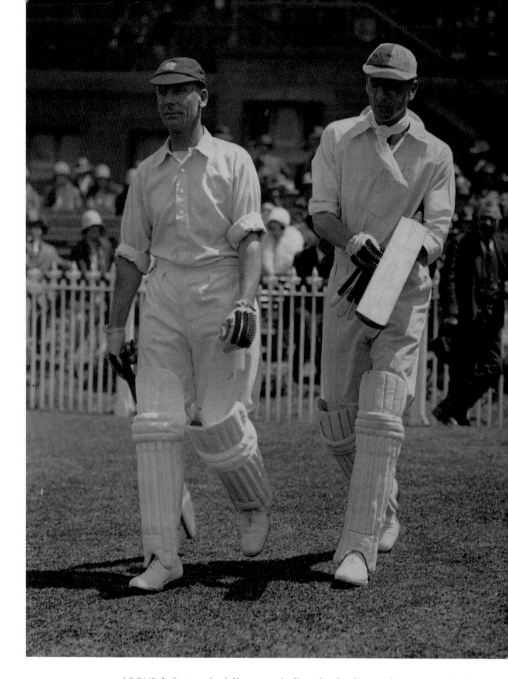

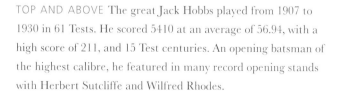

ABOVE Infamous bodyline captain Douglas Jardine and team-mate Jack Hobbs go out to open the Fifth Test in 1929 at the MCG. Match Scores: England 519 (J.B.Hobbs 142, M.Leyland 137, E.H.Hendren 95) and 257 (J.B.Hobbs 65, M.W.Tait 54, M.Leyland 53, T.W.Wall 5 for 66); Australia 491 (D.G.Bradman 123, W.M.Woodfull 102, A.G.Fairfax 65, G.Geary 5 for 105) and 287 for 5 (J.Ryder 57, W.A.Oldfield 48, A.A.Jackson 46). Australia won by 5 wickets.

OPPOSITE TOP LEFT AND RIGHT Johnny Taylor, the stalwart Test cricketer of the 1920s. He played from 1920 to 1926. Seen here in his A.I.F. cap for the unofficial 'Test'matches played in England after the start of The Great War. He played in 20 Tests, scoring 997 runs at 35.6, with a top score of 108.

OPPOSITE BELOW A wet Sydney Cricket Ground. This gives a good indication of what the batsman faced in the days of uncovered pitches when the wicket dried out.

TOP AND ABOVE The great Jack Hobbs played from 1907 to 1930 in 61 Tests. He scored 5410 at an average of 56.94, with a high score of 211, and 15 Test centuries. An opening batsman of the highest calibre, he featured in many record opening stands with Herbert Sutcliffe and Wilfred Rhodes.

OPPOSITE Archie Jackson and Bill Woodfull going out to open the batting in the Fourth Test at Adelaide in the 1928–29. Jackson scored a majestic 164 on debut. Match Scores: England 334 (W.R.Hammond 119, J.B.Hobbs 74, H.Sutcliffe 64, C.V.Grimmett 5 for 102) and 383 (W.R.Hammond 177, D.R.Jardine 98, M.W.Tait 47, R.K.Oxenham 4 for 67); Australia 369 (A.A.Jackson 164, J.Ryder 63, D.G.Bradman 40, J.C.White 5 for 130, M.W.Tait 4 for 77) and 336 (J.Ryder 87, D.G.Bradman 38, A.F.Kippax 51, J.C.White 8 for 126). England won by 12 runs.

ABOVE Jack Ryder, an Australian captain and later selector played 20 in Tests from 1920 to 1929, captaining the debut series of Jackson and Bradman, scored 1394 runs at an average of 51.62, with a high score of 201 not out. He was also an occasional bowler, snaring 17 Test wickets. When his playing career was over he continued to devote much of his time to the development of young players, and was also a selector from 1946 to 1970.

LEFT Such was the dominance over Australia in the 1928/29 series, England's feared fast bowler even excelled with the bat. Seen here going out to bat with A.P.F. Chapman at the Sydney Cricket Ground in the Second Test, 1928. Match Scores: Australia 253 (W.M.Woodfull 68, W.A.Oldfield 41, G.Geary 5 for 35) and 397 (H.S.T.L.Hendry 112, W.M.Woodfull 111, J.Ryder 79, O.E.Nothling 44, M.W.Tate 4 for 99); England 636 (W.R.Hammond 251, E.H.Hendren 74, G.Geary 66, H.Larwood 43, J.B.Hobbs 40, D.Blackie 4 for 148) and 16 for 2. England won by 8 wickets. Wally Hammond was the undisputed star of this series, scoring 905 at an average of 113.12. His scores in that series were: 44, 28, 251, 200, 32, 119, 177, 38 and 16.

'Mutt' and 'Jeff' as they called themselves. W.M.Woodfull (left) and W.H.Ponsford, both of Victoria, go out to open Australia's innings of 695 at the Oval in 1930. Their stand contributed 159. In 35 Tests Woodfull scored 2300 at 46.00. He captained Australia in 25 Tests scoring seven centuries. In Shield cricket he scored 3615 at 66.94. He played in 29 Tests from 1924 to 1934, and scored 2122 runs at an

1930 – 1939

3

1930

THE 1930S WAS A DECADE OF ECONOMIC DEPRESSION and gradual recovery, political fascism and the growth of intense nationalism — especially in Europe. The Australian public looked to its sporting heroes for respite from the realities of this bleak decade — Phar Lap in horseracing, Walter Lindrum in billiards and Hubert Opperman in cycling, to name a few — but most importantly, to the feats of Donald Bradman on the cricket fields of Australia and England. The NSW batsman, just 21 years-old at the beginning of the decade, scored 4625 Test runs during the 1930s at an average of 102.77 runs per innings.

With 19 centuries to his credit during the 1930s, Don Bradman's fame transcended the sport that he mastered.

Australia opened the decade with the Ashes tour of England in May 1930 under the captaincy of Bill Woodfull. Bradman's reputation from the 1928–29 Ashes series preceded him in England, but local critics openly stated that he would be found wanting on the softer

> *The West Indies may have been an eclectic group of Caribbean countries but they were a united cricket team*

English wickets. Bradman silenced them with scores of 236, 185 and 252 not out and 191 in the lead-up matches before the first Test at Trent Bridge. However, despite Bradman's 131 (after his first innings failure) England won the opening Test of the series by 93 runs. In the second Test at Lords, Bradman scored 254 and Woodfull 155 as Australia won by 7 wickets. But the best was yet to come.

In the third Test of the 1930 Ashes series, Don Bradman became the first player to score over 300 runs in a day's play. The master batsman scored 105 before lunch, then another 115 before tea before ending the day on 309. Bradman's final score of 334 was made up of 46 fours, lasted 383 minutes and mesmerised cricket fans in two nations who had hung to his every run via newspaper and radio news reports. The match was drawn, as was the rain-interrupted fourth Test at Old Trafford, before the Ashes were won in emphatic fashion in the fifth Test at The Oval. Australia responded to England's first innings total of 405 with a healthy 695 after a century to Bill Ponsford and a double century to Bradman. Left-arm spinner Percy Hornibrook took 7/92 as England crashed to an innings and 39 run defeat.

But it was Bradman who was the hero of the tour, and on his return to Australia aboard the *Oronsay* in October 1930, promoters took the unprecedented step of flying him from Adelaide to Melbourne and then onto Sydney so that he could make guest appearances at shops, halls and local cinemas. Don Bradman was not just a cricketing phenomenon ... he was already an Australian icon.

In the summer of 1930–31, Australia hosted the first tour by a West Indian cricket team. Many Australians didn't even know where the West Indies were — other than it was British — but the Australian Board of Control struggled with the realities of the team's 'mix race' squad. Following the existing protocol of the day, approval had to be sought from the Department of Home Affairs to allow the 11 black members of the team into the country but administrators erred, and quickly faced a team revolt, when they booked the squad into separate hotels based on racial lines. The West Indies may have been an eclectic group of Caribbean countries but they were a united cricket team … black or white. Australia won the first four Tests of the series but the visitors won the fifth in Sydney by 30 runs after a brave declaration and first innings centuries to Freddie Martin (123) and George Headley (105). Bradman proved that he was human after all when he was bowled for a duck as Australia failed to score the 251 needed for victory.

England's bowlers terrorised the Australians and the visitors won the match by 10 wickets.

Twelve months later, the South African cricket team visited Australia for the first time since 1910–11. Bradman scored centuries in Australia's three Test victories at the beginning of the series before posting a record 299 not out — the highest score recorded in Australia — in a 10 wicket victory in the fourth Test in Adelaide (Queenslander Hugh 'Pud' Thurlow was run out as Bradman went for the 300th run). Australia completed the 5-0 rout in a rain-ravaged fifth Test in Melbourne. The home side's 153 was enough to record an innings and 72 runs victory, with South Africa bowled out for scores of 36 and 45.

The 1932-33 Ashes series or Bodyline series, as it became known, has become part of Australian folklore. It tested relations between the two countries and came close to being abandoned. The tactics employed by English captain Douglas Jardine to limit Bradman's ability to score runs by bowling at the batsman ('leg-theory' he called it) was given lethal velocity and accuracy by pace bowlers Harold Larwood, Bill Voce and Gubby Allen. Bradman missed the first Test through illness and despite a magnificent 187 by Stan McCabe, England's bowlers terrorised the Australians and the visitors won the match by 10 wickets. 'The Don' was bowled for 0 in the explosive second Test in Melbourne but his century in the second innings and Bill O'Reilly's bowling (5/63 and 5/66) resulted in a 111 run win to the Australians. The series teetered towards cancellation in the third Test in Adelaide after batsman Bert Oldfield suffered a fractured skull (this incident led to Bill Woodfull's famous comment to the England managers that 'there are two teams out there on the oval. One is playing cricket, the other is not.') The enmity between the two teams continued throughout the series, resulting in a 'cable war' between the Australian Board of Control and the MCC. But Jardine's tactics worked; Bradman never scored another century in the series and England won the final two Tests — and the Ashes.

Throughout the later half of 1933, the Australian Board of Control discussed with the MCC the issue of banning 'bodyline' bowling in the proposed Ashes series in England the following year. The Board sanctioned the tour only on the assurance from the MCC that the type of bowling described as 'a direct attack by the bowler on the batsman' and that was 'against the spirit of the game' would not happen again. When Bill Woodfull's

1939

1930

Australian team arrived in England the following May, spin bowling dominated play. Australia won the first Test at Nottingham by 238 runs after spinner Bill O'Reilly took 7/54 in the second innings.

England won the second Test at Lords by an innings and 38 runs after middle-order centuries to Leyland and Ames. With the third Test finishing in a draw, Bradman (304) and Bill Ponsford (181) boosted Australia's first innings total to 584 in the drawn fourth Test at Headingly. The Ashes was ultimately decided in the fifth Test at The Oval when Bradman (244) and Bill Ponsford (266) posted a record 451 partnership (for any wicket!) to set up Australia's mammoth 562 run victory. The 'bodyline' issue was dead and buried.

Bradman's first Test as captain was a memorable one for all the wrong reasons

After a relatively quiet tour, Don Bradman had delivered when it mattered most but the legendary batsman almost lost his life when he was hospitalised with a burst appendix in September. Post operative complications saw his life hang in the balance (Sir Charles Kingsford Smith offered to fly Bradman's wife Jesse to England, but she later sailed to her husband's bedside). Although he recovered, he missed the 1934-35 domestic season and ruled himself out of the tour of South Africa the following year. Health issues would dominate the remainder of his playing career.

Vic Richardson led an Australian team minus Bradman (unavailable) and Ponsford and Woodfull (both retired) to South Africa in 1935–36. Described as one of the happiest tours ever to leave these shores, Australia was undefeated in South Africa, winning 13 of its 16 matches. Richardson led a champion team with centuries from Jack Fingleton, Bill Brown, Stan McCabe and Arthur Chipperfield filling the breach left by Bradman's absence. Australia won the five-Test series 4-nil, with bowler Clarrie Grimmett capturing an incredible 44 wickets (23 in the last two Tests) in the series.

Having captained South Australia to Sheffield Shield victory during the comeback season from illness, Don Bradman was appointed Australian Test captain in November 1936 for the coming Ashes series. Bradman's first Test as captain was a memorable one for all the wrong reasons. Australia was bowled out for 9/58 in the second innings (bowler Ernie McCormick did not bat after coming down with lumbago!) on a wet Brisbane wicket to start the series in the worst possible way — a 322 run loss. When England won the second Test in Sydney by an innings and 22 runs (Wally Hammond scored a double century), Australia was facing an Ashes defeat on home soil.

After Australia fell to 6/130 on a good wicket on the first afternoon of the third Test in Melbourne, the Ashes appeared lost. When the rain came, Australia declared at 9/200 and bowled England out for 76 (Morris Sievers took 5/21 and Bill O'Reilly 3/28). Bradman showed his astuteness as captain when he dropped himself and Jack Fingleton down the order until the pitch dried. The pair put on a 346 run partnership (Bradman 270 and Fingleton 136) in Australia's second innings total of 564 — scores which proved the final difference between the two teams. Bradman scored a double century in Adelaide and a century in Melbourne as Australia claimed an exciting 3-2 series victory to retain the Ashes.

In 1937 New Zealand stopped off in Australia on their return from a 1-nil loss in the three-Test series against England but only played matches against three state teams — NSW, Victoria and South Australia — to recoup financial losses suffered on the tour. Australia looked to 1940 as a possible maiden Test series against the Kiwis but for the time being, the defence of the Ashes in the northern hemisphere summer of 1938 was the country's number one priority.

The visitors crawled to 5/107 as the light faded in the late afternoon on the final day of play

The 1938 Ashes series produced a run-fest in the first two Tests. England's batsmen posted three centuries and a double century in the first innings of the opening Test at Trent Bridge but the match was saved after a fighting 232 by Stan McCabe and second innings centuries from Bradman and Brown. It was a similar story in the second Test at Lords; Wally Hammond's double century was answered by 206 from Brown and 102 not out by Bradman, and the match finished in another draw. With the entire third Test of the series washed out, the Ashes were decided in a rain-marred fourth Test at Headingly. Bradman's 103 set up a narrow first innings lead, and when England was bowled out for 123 Australia needed only 105 for victory. The visitors crawled to 5/107 as the light faded in the late afternoon on the final day of play. The English crowd cheered for Bradman after the Ashes win, but the real hero was Bill O'Reilly who captured ten wickets in the match.

History shows that the fifth of the series at The Oval was the final Ashes Test for eight years. England though, had something to prove in the 'dead rubber' and records fell instead of wickets as the home team scored 7 declared for a record 903 runs. Opener Len Hutton led the way with 364 runs — surpassing Don Bradman's Test record score of 334 — after 13 hours and 20 minutes at the crease. Other records included a 382 run partnership between Hutton and Maurice Leyland and the figures of bowler Leslie Fleetwood-Smith, who finished the match with 1/298 — more than Australia scored in either innings.

On June 22, 1939 former Australian captain 'Monty' Nobel died, age 67. The first cricketer to have a grandstand named after him at the Sydney Cricket Ground (it opened the previous year), Nobel represented an innocent age that was soon to be swept away by the tide of history. War was inevitable in Europe and by the final months of the decade, the world was engulfed by a second World War.

1939

ABOVE LEFT Don Bradman and Stan McCabe on arrival in England on the 1930 tour. Bradman broke all records on tour with a series aggregate of 974 runs from just 7 innings at an average of 139.14, with a then world record highest Test score of 334. His series scores were: 8, 131, 254, 1, 334, 14 and 232. It truly was a case of all or nothing.

LEFT 'Yabba', the rabbit-hawker, whose barbed wit made him a legendary barracker on The Hill at the Sydney Cricket Ground. He had a voice that carried across the ground, and was a great favourite there for years.

ABOVE RIGHT Archie Jackson in 1930. The tour was not a fulfillment of the promise he had earlier shown. It became evident later that the disease that cut short his life within a few years had already taken hold.

OPPOSITE TOP The 1930 Australians in England at a reception for them, held at Australia House in London.

OPPOSITE BOTTOM His Majesty King George V shaking hands with the Australian players prior to the Second Test match at Lord's in June, 1934. Match Scores: England 440 (L.E.G.Ames 120, M.Leyland 109, C.F.Walters 82, T.W.Wall 4 for 108); Australia 284 (W.A.Brown 105, H.Verity 7 for 61) and 118 (W.M.Woodfull 43, H.Verity 8 for 43). England won by an innings and 38 runs. Of the 15 wickets Verity took in this match, he took 14 in one day.

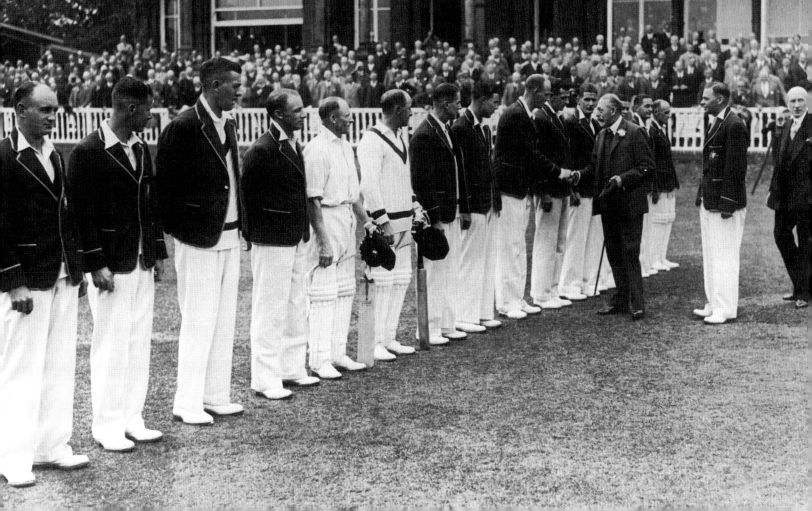

ABOVE The Australian team are welcomed on their arrival at Victoria Station, London in 1930. Left to right: S.J.McCabe, A.Fairfax (behind), D.G.Bradman, P.Hornibrook, T.W.Wall, C.W.Walker, A.F.Kippax, A.P.F.Chapman, A.Hurwood, A.Jackson, T.Howard, Field Marshall Viscount Lord Plumer, W.M.Woodfull, Lord Decies, Mr.W.L.Kelly.

BELOW The English team take the field against Australia in the Third Test in July 1930. From left to right they are: H.Larwood, H.Sutcliffe, G.Geary, W.R.Hammond, K.S.Duleepsinhji, R.Tyldesley, M.W.Tate (partly hidden), G.Duckworth, J.B.Hobbs, A.P.F.Chapman, M.Leyland. Australia batted on day one, and by days end Bradman had scored 309. He scored 105 before lunch, 115 between lunch and tea and 89 between tea and stumps. He must have been tired in the last session.

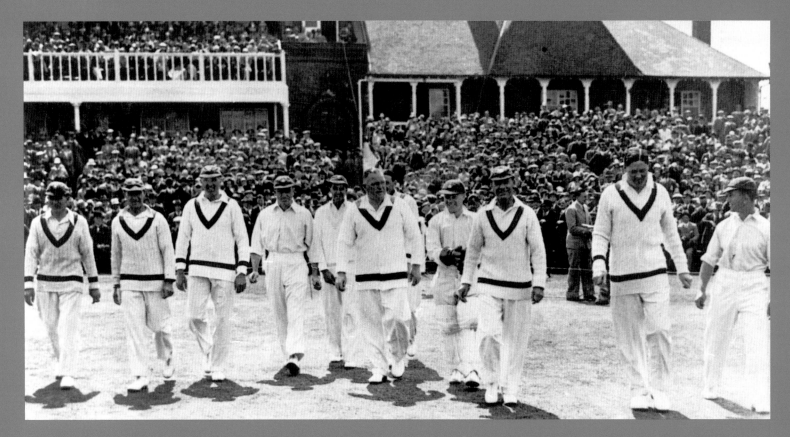

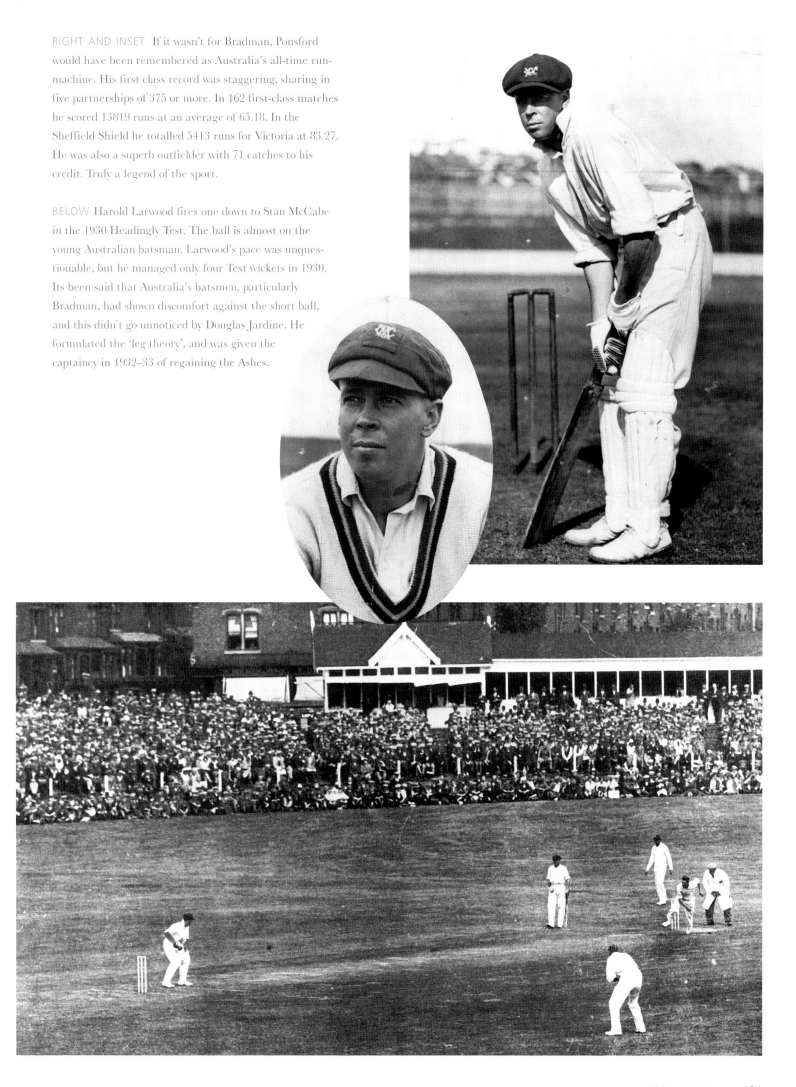

RIGHT AND INSET If it wasn't for Bradman, Ponsford would have been remembered as Australia's all-time run-machine. His first class record was staggering, sharing in five partnerships of 375 or more. In 162 first-class matches he scored 13819 runs at an average of 65.18. In the Sheffield Shield he totalled 5413 runs for Victoria at 83.27. He was also a superb outfielder with 71 catches to his credit. Truly a legend of the sport.

BELOW Harold Larwood fires one down to Stan McCabe in the 1930 Headingly Test. The ball is almost on the young Australian batsman. Larwood's pace was unquestionable, but he managed only four Test wickets in 1930. Its been said that Australia's batsmen, particularly Bradman, had shown discomfort against the short ball, and this didn't go unnoticed by Douglas Jardine. He formulated the 'leg theory', and was given the captaincy in 1932–33 of regaining the Ashes.

*...it was often
said Archie Jackson would have
been better than Bradman*

Tragic New South Wales and
Australian batsman, Archie
Jackson, often said he would
have been better than
Bradman. He was certainly far
more elegant and attractive in
his stroke play. He died of
Tuberculosis at the age of 23
in 1933.

ABOVE The 1930 Australia team in England, who regained the Ashes after the dismal effort in the 'home' series of 1928/29. Left to right, Standing: S.J.McCabe, A.Hurwood, T.W.Wall, P.M.Hornibrook, E.L.A'Beckett, A.F.Kippax, C.V.Grimmett, W.A.Oldfield. Seated: D.G.Bradman, W.H.Ponsford, V.Y.Richardson, W.M.Woodfull (Captain), C.W.Walker, A.Jackson, A.Fairfax.

BOTTOM Ponsford batting for Victoria against New South Wales at the SCG in the 1930s. Shown here on his way to a score of 200, with Oldfield behind the wickets and O'Reilly at first slip in a Sheffield Shield match.

RIGHT Monty Noble shown in the 1930s, finished his Test career in 1909 and began a long and illustrious career in administration. He also gained wide popularity as a lecturer on cricket throughout Australia.

ABOVE Len Darling, the dashing left-handed batsman, with a fine array of shots, played in 12 Tests from 1933 to 1937, in which he scored 474 runs at an average of 27.88. While his Test appearances were few, he played 100 first class games, scoring 5780 runs at an average of 42.5, which included 16 centuries with a high score of 188. Shown here playing for Victoria, turns one from Cheetham (New South Wales) to leg in a Sheffield Shield match.

ABOVE RIGHT Len Darling, in an unusal situation of pulling a Bradman delivery to the fence for four in a Sheffield Shield match for South Australia against New South Wales in 1934.

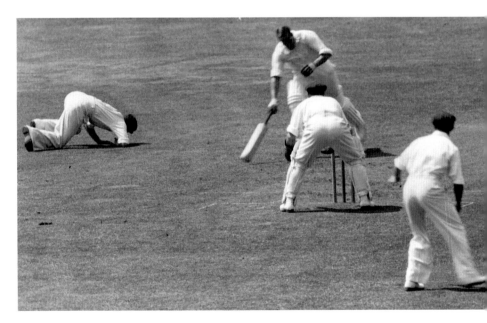

ABOVE Len Darling, throws himself on the ground when fielding a hot return in the Third Test at Manchester in 1934. Bradman is the other fielder, while Oldfield is behind the stumps.

LEFT Archie Jackson and Don Bradman going out to bat during the third day's play in the Fifth Test in 1930 at The Oval. Their stand of 243 for the fourth wicket, turned the match Australia's way. Match Scores: England 405 (H.Sutcliffe 161, R.E.S.Wyatt 64, K.S.Duleepsinhji 50, J.B.Hobbs 47, C.V.Grimmett 4 for 135) and 251 (W.R.Hammond 60, H.Sutcliffe 54, K.S.Duleepsinhji 46, P.M.Hornibrook 7 for 92); Australia 695 (D.G.Bradman 232, W.H.Ponsford 110, A.A.Jackson 73, W.M.Woodfull 54, S.J.McCabe 54, A.G.Fairfax 53, I.A.R.Peebles 6 for 204). Australia won by an innings and 39 runs.

BELOW New South Wales v Queensland at the Sydney Cricket Ground, January, 1930. Bradman has just pulled a Thurlow delivery to the square leg boundary to make a world record highest score in one innings in a first class match, 452 not out, breaking Bill Ponsford's previous record of 437.

Bradman executing his famous cover drive at the SCG for New South Wales against England during the Bodyline tour of 1932–33.

ABOVE The end of the Fifth Test at the Oval in 1934. Going into the match the teams were one win each and two draws. Australia needed to win to wrest back the Ashes after the Bodyline debacle. Match scores: Australia 701 (W.H.Ponsford 266, D.G.Bradman 244, W.M.Woodfull 49, W.A.S.Oldfield 42, W.E.Bowes 4 for 164, G.O.B.Allen 4 for 170) and 327 (D.G.Bradman 77, S.J.McCabe 70, H.I.Ebeling 41, W.E.Bowes 5 for 55, E.W.Clark 5 for 98); England 321 (M.Leyland 110, C.F.Walters 64) and 145 (W.R.Hammond 43, C.V.Grimmett 5 for 64). Australia won by 562 runs.

ABOVE Bradman and a friend, 'Curly' Jones in the 1931-32 season.

OPPOSITE R.E.S.Wyatt (left) and W.M.Woodfull (right) toss prior to the England versus Australia Third Test at manchester in 1934. England batted first and amassed an enormous score of 627, however their captain Wyatt was bowled by O'Reilly for a duck.

ABOVE During Arthur Mailey's goodwill cricket tour to the US and Canada in 1932. It was also Bradman's honeymoon trip. Hollywood actors take time off filming Fu Man Chu to have a photograph taken with the Australian players. Left to right, Top: Boris Karloff. Back Row: A.Mailey, unknown actor, V.Richardson, the Director. Centre: H.Carter. Third Row: E.Rofe, R.Nutt, W.Ives, S.McCabe. Second Row: P.Carney, L.Fleetwood-Smith, Myrna Loy, K.Tolhurst, A.Kippax, D.Bradman. Front Row: Desmond Roberts, unknown actor, Charles Aubrey Smith.

LEFT Don and Jessie Bradman with Mr and Mrs A.K.Bell in Scotland in 1934. Mr Bell was the head of the firm renowned for the whisky bearing his name.

ABOVE Archie Jackson with some of the hostesses at a reception for the Australian cricket team in London in 1930 at which the Dowager Countess of Darnley and the committee of the International Sportsmen's Club were hosts.

BELOW Arthur Mailey, Boris Karloff, Leslie Howard, Mrs Howard, Desmond Roberts and, Victor Richardson in the USA in 1932 as part of Arthur Mailey's touring team.

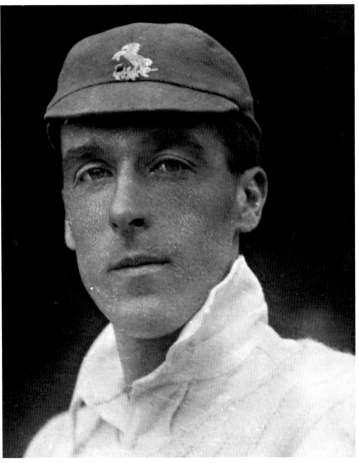

ABOVE Australia are playing Worcestershire on the 1930 tour of England. The Australian team are in the field with Clarrie Grimmett bowling. The tourists won this match by an innings and 165 runs, with Bradman top-scoring with 236 and Grimmet taking 4 for 38 and 5 for 46.

LEFT Frank E.Woolley during the 1930 Test series in England against the Australians. A left handed batsman, he played in 64 Tests over 25 years from 1909 to 1934, scoring 3283 runs at an average of 36.07, with a high score of 154 against South Africa in 1929.

OPPOSITE TOP England's Ames playing Clarrie Grimmett's bowling for Australia on the third day of the Fifth Test in 1934 at The Oval. Grimmett claimed 5 for 64 during England's second innings.

OPPOSITE BOTTOM Jack Ryder, who played 20 Tests from 1920–21 to 1928–29, scored 1394 runs at an average of 51.62, with a high score of 201 against England in 1925. He also took 17 wickets, at 43.7, used mostly as a change bowler. He was captain of Australia for the 1928–29 tour by England's Chapman side. They lost the series 4-1, however were greatly under-strengthed minus Collins, Bardsley, Macartney, Taylor and Mailey who had all retired, Arthur Richardson was in England and Gregory and Kelleway were injured during the First Test and would take no more part in the series. As an 87 year-old he attended the Centenary Test in Melbourne in 1977, at which he was the oldest player present. Unfortunately he took ill a few days later and passed away.

ABOVE Members of the 1932 New South Wales team relax in the dressing room. Among them is Don Bradman (far left with feet over the seats) and Jack Fingleton (third player seated from right).

LEFT The Kippax team that toured North Queensland in 1931, left to right, Back Row: P.Withers, F.Conway, H.Hooker, W.Ives, A.Fairfax, W.Bill, K.Rigg. Front Row: S.McCabe, A.Jackson, A.Kippax (captain), E.L.Waddy (manager), D.Bradman. Some of the centres they traveled to included, Cairns, Innisfail, Townsville, Ayr, Bowen and Mackay. Bradman scored four centuries and a 90 in nine innings on the tour.

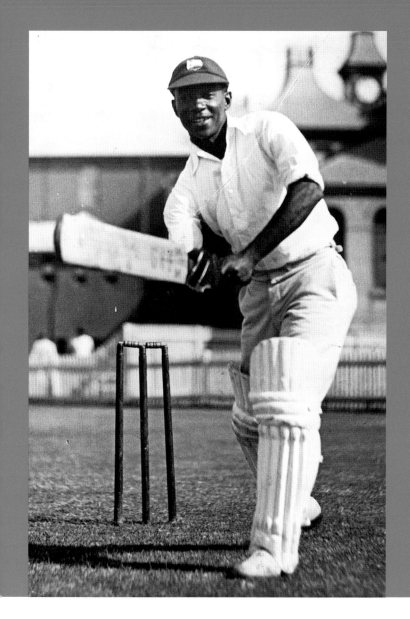

LEFT AND ABOVE   West Indian George Headley was once described by London newspapers as the Bradman of the West Indies. He was a member of the West Indian team that toured Australia 1930–31, losing the Test series 4-1. In the Third Test, he scored 102 and became the first West Indian cricketer to ever score a century against Australia.

BELOW South Africa toured Australia in 1931–32 and playing a five match Test series, losing 5-0. The First Test of that series, played on November 27, 28 and December 2 and 3, was the first ever Test match to be played on the Brisbane Cricket Ground. Up to that time the Tests had been played at the Brisbane Exhibition Ground. The South African team are, left to right, Back Row: A.J.Bell, C.L.Vincent, K.F.Vitjoen, E.L.Dalton, S.S.L.Steyne, S.H.Curnow, L.S.Brown. Centre Row: J.A.J.Christy, H.W.Taylor, Mr. Tandy (manager), H.B.Cameron, Q.McMillan, N.A.Quinn. Front Row: X.Balaskas, E.A.Van der Merwe, B.Mitchell.

ABOVE The MCC team in 1932 aboard the ship, the SS *Orontes*.

LEFT Larwood, Voce, Leyland aboard ship while coming to Australia for the 1932 Ashes series.

Tensions were simmering after the first two Tests, but emotions boiled over in this most dramatic of matches

ABOVE The Douglas Jardine English team of 1932–33 photographed at Adelaide prior to the Third Test. Tensions were simmering after the first two Tests, but emotions boiled over in this most dramatic of matches.

LEFT Australian Bert Ironmonger bowled by Quinn in the First Test in Brisbane of the 1931–32 series against South Africa. Match Scores: Australia 450 (D.G.Bradman 226, W.M.Woodfull 76, W.A.Oldfield 56, A.J.Bell 4 for 120); South Africa 170 (B.Mitchell 58, H.Ironmonger 5 for 42) and 117 (T.W.Wall 5 for 14, H.Ironmonger 4 for 44). Australia won by an innings and 163 runs.

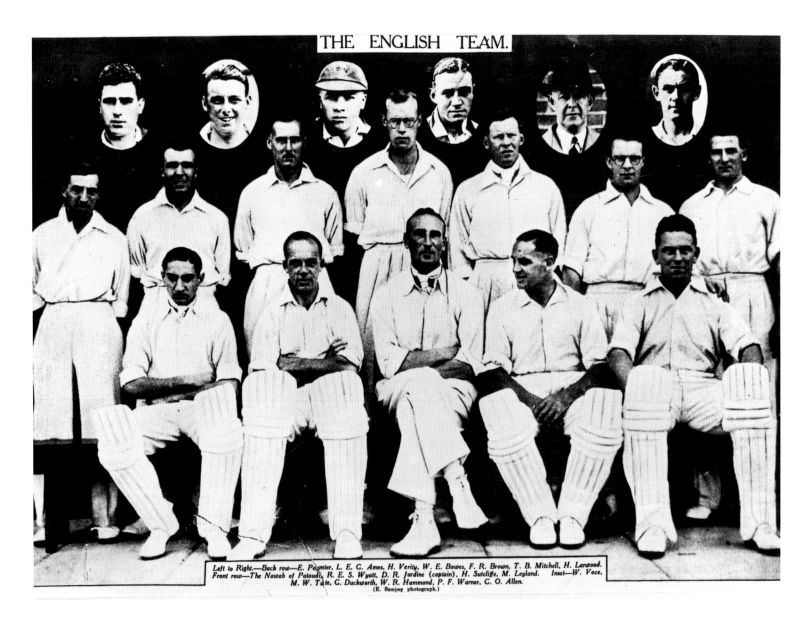

Left to Right.—Back row—E. Paynter, L. E. G. Ames, H. Verity, W. E. Bowes, F. R. Brown, T. B. Mitchell, H. Larwood.
Front row—The Nawab of Pataudi, R. E. S. Wyatt, D. R. Jardine (captain), H. Sutcliffe, M. Leyland. Inset—W. Voce,
M. W. Tate, G. Duckworth, W. R. Hammond, P. F. Warner, G. O. Allen.
(E. Sampey photograph.)

ABOVE The English team that toured Australia in 1932–33 in the series that would forever be remembered as bodyline. Left to right, Inset: W.Voce, M.W.Tate, G.Duckworth, W.R.Hammond, P.F.Warner, G.O.Allen. Standing: E.Paynter, L.E.G.Ames, H.Verity, W.E.Bowes, F.R.Brown, T.B.Mitchell, H.Larwood. Sitting: The Nawab of Pataudi, R.E.S.Wyatt, D.R.Jardine (Captain), H.Sutcliffe, M.Leyland.

LEFT The start of the unhappiest series of all. W.M.Woodfull (left) and D.R.Jardine toss before the First Test of the bodyline summer at Sydney 1932–33. Woodfull won the toss, as Jardine's expression would suggest. Match scores: Australia 360 (S.J.McCabe 187, V.Y.Richardson 49, H.Larwood 5 for 96, W.Voce 4 for 110) and 164 (J.H.W.Fingleton 40, H.Larwood 5 for 28); England 524 (H.Sutcliffe 194, W.R.Hammond 112, Nawab of Pataudi 102) and 1 for 0. England won by 10 wickets.

ABOVE Adelaide Oval during the Third Test of the Bodyline series. This match was played amid ugly scenes when Australian wicket-keeper W.A.Oldfield was struck on the head from a delivery by English fast bowler, Harold Larwood. Oldfield staggered a few metres from the wicket and then fell to the ground. With the agitated crowd booing continuously, serious trouble looked imminent, but the unrest went no further.

RIGHT W.M.Woodfull clutches his chest after being struck over the heart by a ball from Larwood in a sickening blow during the same match. English fieldsman Bill Bowes doesn't appear overly worried by the developments. Match Scores: England 341 (M.Leyland 83, R.E.S.Wyatt 78, E.Paynter 77, H.Verity 45, T.W.Wall 5 for 72) and 412 (W.R.Hammond 85, L.E.G.Ames 69, D.R.Jardine 56, R.E.S.Wyatt 49, M.Leyland 42, H.Verity 40, W.J.O'Reilly 4 for 79); Australia 222 (W.H.Ponsford 85, W.A.Oldfield 41, G.O.B.Allen 4 for 71) and 193 (W.M.Woodfull 73, D.G.Bradman 66, G.O.B.Allen 4 for 50, H.Larwood 4 for 71). England won by 338 runs.

*... the Australian batsman often given
no choice but to fend the short leg-side
deliveries to the waiting field.*

ABOVE LEFT Stan McCabe is injured in yet another bodyline attack by the English pacemen. His batting partner, Don Bradman is coming over to check on him.

ABOVE RIGHT Bill Voce, who was the fast bowler who partnered Harold Larwood in the Bodyline Series. Voce played 27 Tests for England from 1929–30 to 1946–47, capturing 98 wickets at an average of 27.88. During the bodyline series he captured 15 wickets at 27.13, with his best return in the First Test at Sydney when he took 4 for 110 and 2 for 54, with England winning the match by 10 wickets.

LEFT Bert Ironmonger, who played in 14 Tests from 1928–29 to 1932–33, took 74 wickets at an average of 17.97, with a career best of 7 for 23 against the West Indies in the Fourth Test at Melbourne in the 1930/31 tour to Australia. In the batting stakes, however, he was a real 'bunny',scoring just 42 runs at 2.62.

ABOVE Ponsford, during a Sheffield Shield match at the SCG in 1932, between Victoria and New South Wales. Bert Oldfield is the wicketkeeper and Bill O'Reilly at first slip.

RIGHT Johnny Taylor, the New South Wales and Australian right hand batsman, whose first class career went from 1913–14 to 1926–27. For Australia he played in 20 Tests, scored 997 runs at an average of 35.6, with a high score of 108, his only Test century. In all first class matches he played 135 matches, scored 6274 runs at an average of 33.37, with a high score of 180.

In the batting stakes, Bert Ironmonger was a real 'bunny', scoring just 42 runs at 2.62

Bill O'Reilly, was, until Shane Warne came along, arguably the greatest spin bowler the game had ever produced. At 6ft 2in tall, he released the ball that was almost fast-medium pace, bouncing ferociously on the hard pitches of the day. He bowled a mixture of leg-breaks, especially top-spinners and googles, and was an intimidating opponent. He played for Australia in 27 Tests from 1927/28 to 1945/46, took 144 wickets at an average of 22.59, with career best figures of 7/54 in an innings and 11/129 in a match.

Touring England in 1934 and 1938 his respective figures were 118 wickets at 16.02 and 104 wickets at 16.59. In first class matches he played in 135 matches, took 774 wickets at 16.6, taking 10 wickets in a match on 17 occasions. He also topped the Sydney grade cricket averages 12 times, taking 962 wickets at 9.44. He was one of cricket's larger than life personalities, as a player, a character and in later life as an outspoken writer on the game. When Bill O'Reilly passed away in 1992, Don Bradman said 'he was the greatest bowler he had either faced or watched.' Another player, Jack Fingleton said of him, 'he was a flurry of limbs, fire and steel-edged temper.' Off the field his gruffness was mitigated by his intelligence, great wit and the twinkling eyes.

Bill O'Reilly was one of cricket's larger than life personalities, as a player, a character and in later life as an outspoken writer on the game

one of our very best cricketers, a supremely eloquent batsman, and a modest person who would shun publicity at all costs

ABOVE LEFT A.P.Freeman, was a slow bowler, who was just starting his career when the First World War broke out. He toured Australia in 1924–25, played for England in 12 Tests from 1924–25 to 1929, took 66 wickets at an average of 25.86, with best figures of 7/71 in the fourth Test against South Africa at Old Trafford in 1929.

TOP RIGHT Patsy Hendren, who toured Australia with the English teams of 1920, 1924–25 and 1928–29. He was a right-handed batsman who played for England from 1920–21 to 1934–35, played in 51 Tests, scored 3,525 runs at an average of 47.63, with a top score of 205 against the West Indies in 1930 in the Second Test at Port of Spain.

RIGHT W.H.Ponsford, lived until he was 90 in 1991. When he passed away he was Australia's oldest living Test cricketer and the last survivor of H.L.Collins' 1926 team to England. He played first-class cricket from 1920–21 to 1933–34 and for Australia from 1924 to 1934. In his 29 Tests he scored 2122 runs at an average of 48.22, with a high score of 266, scoring 7 centuries in total. His first class career spanned 162 matches, scoring 13819 runs at 65.18, with a top score of 437, and in all he scored 47 centuries. In only his fourth innings in a first-class game he scored a world record 429 runs in just 477 minutes. The Victorian team that match amassed the first four-figure total in first-class cricket, with 1059. Ponsford had gone to the wicket with his side at 3 for 200 and was at the crease to hit the 1000th run himself. In a run-scoring spree never before matched his innings (in 1926–27) in order were: 214, 54, 151, 352, 108, 84, 12, 116, 131 and 7, totaling 1229 runs at 122.9; in 1927–28 he scored 133, 437, 202, 38, 336, 6, 2, 63, totaling 1217 at 152.12. The 336 he scored for Victoria against South Australia in January, 1928 was his 11th first-class hundred in consecutive matches. His Test record was interrupted by illness, injury and Bodyline. In 1932–33 he never took a backward step when under fire from Jardine's Englishmen, and by staying in the line of fire he absorbed a lot of punishment. This great Victorian was one of our very best cricketers, a supremely eloquent batsman, who was also colour-blind, a man of few words outside the dressing-room, and a modest person who would shun publicity at all costs.

TOP One of the truly great spinners, Clarrie Grimmett lets one rip against England. He played for Australia in 37 Tests, debuting as a 33 year-old, playing from 1925 to 1936. He took 216 wickets at an average of 24.21, with best figures in an innings of 7/40 against South Africa in the Fourth Test at Johannesburg in 1936 and best figures in a match of 14/199 against the same opponent in the Fourth Test at Adelaide in 1932. His first-class career spanned 31 years from 1911–12 to 1940–41, he played 248 matches, took 1424 wickets at an average of 22.28, with best figures of 10 for 37 in an innings. He was a wonderfully accurate bowler, borne of both physical co-odination and endless practice. He mastered the many variations of spin bowling, the standard legbreak, topspinner, googly and, the flipper. On the 1930 tour to England, he captured 29 wickets, which was a record, and it was agreed that his bowling was at least as important to Australia as was Bradman's batting heroics. In England in 1934 he took 25 wickets, and Bill O'Reilly 28. At 44 years of age, he was considered too old, and was dropped from the Australia side for the 1936–37 Test series against England in Australia, and so the destructive spin partnership of Grimmett and O'Reilly was broken up. He went back to Sheffield Shield, and in the 1939–40 season he captured a phenomenal 73 first-class wickets. One of his last public appearances was at the Centenary Test in Melbourne in 1977.

ABOVE Jack Ryder, playing for Victoria opens his score with a boundary stroke against New South Wales in January of 1932. Behind the stumps is Bert Oldfield, while Bill O'Reilly is at slip.

ABOVE LEFT AND RIGHT Wily left-hander Bert 'Dainty' Ironmonger, a slow-medium left-arm spin bowler, debuted for Australia in Test cricket at age 45. Against the West Indies team of 1930–31 he was extremely successful both for Victoria and Australia . For his state he took 5/87 and 8/31 in a match, while in the four Tests he played he captured 22 wickets at 14.68.

RIGHT Stan McCabe debuted as a 19 year-old for Australia in 1930 and played until 1938, appearing in 39 Tests. He scored 2748 runs at an average of 48.21, which included a high score of 232 against England in the First Test at Nottingham in 1938. His first class career spanned 14 years from 1928 to 1942, during which he scored 11951 runs at 49.39 and scored 29 centuries. During the onslaught that was Bodyline, McCabe scored 385 runs at an average of 42.77. In a stellar career many tributes were bestowed upon him. After his 232 not out against England in 1938, Sir Donald Bradman greeted him on his return to the dressing room with, 'If I could play an innings like that, I'd be a proud man, Stan.' The former Prime Minister, Sir Robert Menzies, who loved watching cricket, said of him, 'One of his great points was that he never bothered about averages; he enjoyed his batting. He was one of the two or three greatest batsmen I ever saw.'

ABOVE W.M.Woodfull gazes on his shattered wicket after being beaten and bowled by the young Queenslander, J.Govan in October of 1932.

RIGHT Bill Woodfull scoring a century in his Testimonial Match. He played for Australia in 35 Tests, from 1926 to 1934, captaining them in 25. He scored 2,300 runs at an average of 46.9, with a high score of 161 against South Africa in the Third Test at Melbourne in 1931–32.

Woodfull maybe wasn't graceful, but he knew the value of footwork. Here he glances Oxenham to leg for two in the Sheffield Shield game for Victoria against Queensland at the Melbourne Cricket Ground in 1933.

ABOVE Spectators, with a fair smattering of youngsters, queue to get into the Sydney Cricket Ground for the First Test of the Bodyline Series of 1932-33.

OPPOSITE BOTTOM Ponsford caught by O'Reilly for Victoria against New South Wales in November, 1933

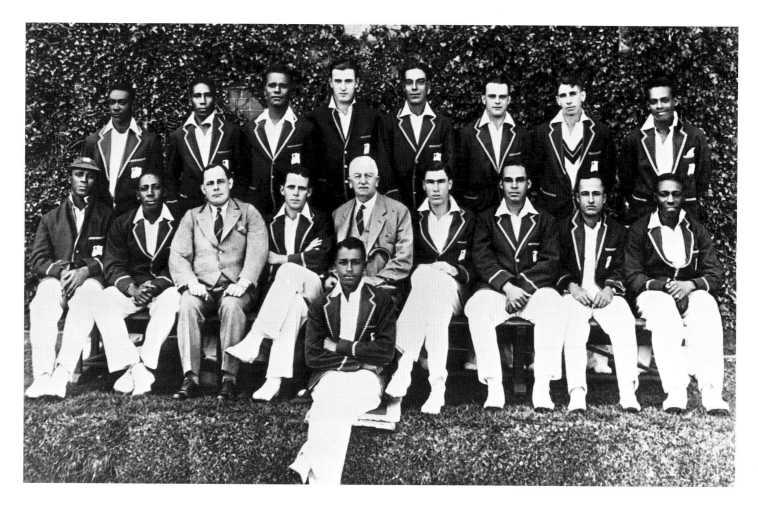

ABOVE The first West Indies cricket team to tour Australia, was the 1930-31. Pictured here, they are, left to right, Standing: G.Headley, C.A.Roach, E.A.C.Hunte, F.I. de Caires, O.S.Scott, I.Barrow, E.L.Hill. Seated: H.C.Griffith, N.N.Constantine, Mr. J.E.Seheult (Assistant Manager), G.C.Grant (Captain), Mr. R.H.Mallett (Manager). L.S.Birkett (Vice-Captain), F.R.Martin, E.L.Bartlett, G.Francis. In Front: J.E.D.Sealey. Australia won the series 4-1. Australia's spinner Clarrie Grimmett was just too good for the Windies, with his figures in the first three Tests: 7-87, 4 for 96, 4 for 54, 4 for 95 and 5 for 49.

ABOVE New South Wales team that played Victoria in January, 1934. Left to right, Standing: W.A.Brown, A.G.Chipperfield, C.J.Hill, H.J.Theak, W.J.O'Reilly, O.W.Bill. Seated: R.Rowe, D.G.Bradman, A.F.Kippax (Captain), J.H.Fingleton, H.C.Chilvers. Bradman scored a quick fire 128 in this game, with the last 118 runs in just 58 minutes. In his last four innings for NSW he had scored 645 runs (187 not out, 77 not out, 253 and 128).

BELOW Bill Woodfull batting in Australia's first match of their 1934 tour in England, against Worcester. The Bill Woodfull led Australian team won the Ashes 2-1, with the other two Tests drawn. Woodfull's run-making efforts in this series, when he scored 228 runs at 28.5, was not up to his previous three tours in England. In 1930, he had scored 345 at an average of 57.5, in 1928/29 he'd scored 491 at 54.55 and in 1926, 306 at 51.0. Ponsford, Bradman and McCabe were the main run-getters in 1934. Ponsford scored 569 runs at 94.83, Bradman 758 at 94.75 and McCabe 483 at 60.37.

RIGHT TOP Oldfield, the Australian wicket-keeper leaps high to take a return from the outfield. Action from the Second Test at Lords in 1934 between Australia and England. Match Scores: England 440 (L.E.G.Ames 120, M.Leyland 109, C.F.Walters 82, T.W.Wall 4 for 108); Australia 284 (W.A.Brown 105, H.Verity 7 for 61) and 118 (W.M.Woodfull 43, H.Verity 8 for 43). England won by an innings and 38 runs.

RIGHT BOTTOM Patsy Hendren and George Geary, who saved the follow on for England at Trent Bridge in the First Test of the 1934 series against Australia, are applauded as they returned to the pavilion. Match Score: Australia 374 (A.G.Chipperfield 99, S.J.McCabe 65, W.H.Ponsford 53, K.Farnes 5 for 102) and 273 for 8 dec (S.J.McCabe 88, W.A.Brown 73, K.Farnes 5 for 77); England 268 (E.H.Hendren 79, H.Sutcliffe 62, G.Geary 53, C.V.Grimmett 5 for 81, W.J.O'Reilly 4 for 75) and 141 (C.F.Walters 46, W.J.O'Reilly 7 for 54). Australia won by 238 runs.

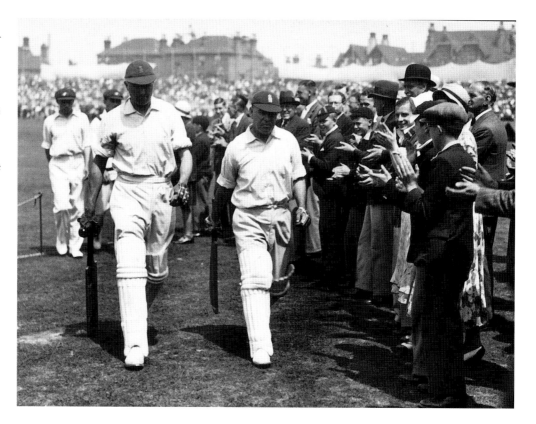

ABOVE Fourth and last day of the Third Test match between England and Australia at Old Trafford, Manchester. Australia's Bill O'Reilly is seen making the stroke to the leg boundary off a ball from Verity that saved the follow-on for his side. He was eventually run out for 18. Match Scores: England 627 for 9 dec (M.Leyland 153, E.H.Hendren 132, L.E.G.Ames 72, H.Sutcliffe 63, G.O.B.Allen 61, H.Verity 60, C.F.Walters 52, W.J.O'Reilly 7 for 189) and 123 for 0 dec (H.Sutcliffe 69, C.F.Walters 50); Australia 491 (S.J.McCabe 137, W.M.Woodfull 73, W.A.Brown 72, H.Verity 4 for 78) and 66 for 1. Match drawn.

BELOW R.E.S.Wyatt (MCC) hits L.O.B.Fleetwood-Smith to leg for two runs in the MCC v Australians clash at Lord's on May 18th, 1934, their first match in London on the Australian 1934 tour.

England players Wyatt and Allen, seen here opening the batting for the MCC against Yorkshire on August, 1934. The match was part of the Scarborough Cricket Festival.

RIGHT Ames (England) drives O'Reilly to the boundary during the Third Test at Old Trafford, Manchester. In a marathon spell in the first innings, O'Reilly took 7 for 189 from 59 overs for Australia. In the same innings Clarrie Grimmett bowled 57 overs for 1 for 122. They sure worked them hard in those days.

BELOW LEFT AND RIGHT As a cricketer Victor Richardson attracted most attention for his excellent fielding. He had speed, agility and very safe hands, which made him valuable in any fielding position. During Bodyline he and Bill Woodfull shared an opening stand of 133 in the Fourth Test at Brisbane. In later life he became a radio commentator on the game.

ABOVE Ponsford gets the ball past Hammond in the slips at Headingly in the Fourth Test in 1934. Bradman and Ponsford put on a record 388 for the fourth wicket. Australia had started the day at 39 for 3 but finished it at 494 for 4. Match Scores: England 200 (C.F.Walters 44, C.V.Grimmett 4 for 57) and 229 for 6 (M.Leyland 49, C.F.Walters 45, W.E.S.Wyatt 44, E.H.Hendren 42);Australia 584 (D.G.Bradman 304, W.H.Ponsford 181, W.E.Bowes 6 for 142). Match drawn.

RIGHT W.H.Ponsford, a tourist to England in 1926, 1930 and 1934. He finished his last tour with the best batting average in the Test Series. He played 7 innings, 1 not out, scored 569 runs at an average of 94.83, and had a high score of 266 in the Fifth Test at The Oval.

Bradman and Ponsford put on a record 388 for the fourth wicket

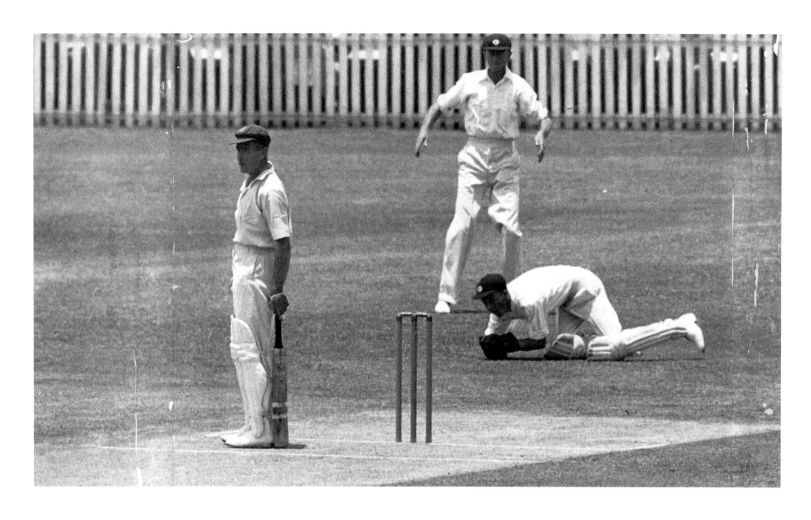

ABOVE Victor Richardson (South Australia) snicks a ball behind, but stands awaiting the umpires decision, in a Sheffield Shield match with Queensland in 1934. He played 19 Tests for Australia from 1924 to 1936, scored 706 runs at an average of 23.53, with a high score of 138 against England in 1924–25 at Melbourne in the Second Test. While at first-class level he played 184 matches 1918/19 to 1937/38, scored 10,727 runs at 37.63, with a high score of 231, which included 27 centuries.

OPPOSITE TOP Patsy Hendren pulls a ball from Australia's Bill O'Reilly during his innings of 42 not out in the Fourth Test of 1934 at Headingly. Match Scores: England 200 (C.F.Walters 44, C.V.Grimmett 4 for 57) and 229 for 6 (M.Leyland 49, C.F.Walters 45, R.E.S.Wyatt 44, E.H.Hendren 42); Australia 584 (D.G.Bradman 304, W.H.Ponsford 181, W.E.Bowes 6 for 142). Match drawn.

OPPOSITE BOTTOM Hendren again, this time making another forceful stroke during his great innings of 132 against Australia in the Third Test at Old Trafford in 1934. Match Scores: England 627 for 9 dec (M.Leyland 153, E.H.Hendren 132, L.E.G.Ames 72, H.Sutcliffe 63, G.o.B.Allen 61, H.Verity 60, C.F.Walters 52, W.J.O'Reilly 7 for 189) and 123 for 0 dec (H.Sutcliffe 69, C.F.Walters 50); Australia 491 (S.J.McCabe 137, W.M.Woodfull 73, W.A.Brown 72, H.Verity 4 for 78) and 66 for 1. Match drawn.

...making another forceful stroke during his great innings of 132 against Australia in the Third Test at Old Trafford

TOP Hendren and Leyland, who both made great scores for England, with 132 and 153 respectively, during the Third Test match at Manchester on the 1934 tour. Leyland is seen batting against Australia's Stan McCabe.

BOTTOM England's Ames hooks a ball from Clarrie Grimmett to the leg boundary. He went on to make a top score of 120. At the conclusion of this Second Test at Lord's in 1934, some of the 30,000 strong crowd rushed across the field and mobbed the players. Match Scores: England 440 (L.E.G.Ames 120, M.Leyland 109, C.F.Walters 82, T.W.Wall 4 for 108); Australia 284 (W.A.Brown 105, H.Verity 7 for 61) and 118 (W.M.Woodfull 43, H.Verity 8 for 43). England won by an innings and 38 runs.

ABOVE LEFT L.S.Darling on his way to 98, hits a ball from J.G.W.Davies to the leg boundary in the match between Australian and Cambridge University at Fenners Ground, Cambridge in May, 1934.

ABOVE RIGHT George Geary of England, whose score of 53 in the First Test at Trent Bridge was the bulk of his series aggregate of 62 in a disappointing 1934 Test series for him.

LEFT B.A.Barnett, wicketkeeper for both Victoria and Australia, played his only four Tests on the 1938 tour of England.

RIGHT Woodfull wins the toss prior to play in the First Test at Trent Bridge in 1934. England's captain is C.F.Walters. Match Scores: Australia 374 (A.G.Chipperfield 99, S.J.McCabe 65, W.H.Ponsford 53, K.Farnes 5 for 102) and 273 for 8 dec (S.J.McCabe 88, W.A.Brown 73, K.Farnes 5 for 77); England 268 (E.H.Hendren 79, H.Sutcliffe 62, G.Geary 53, C.V.grimmett 5 for 81, W.J.O'Reilly 4 for 75) and 141 (C.F.Walters 46, W.J.O'Reilly 7 for 54). Australia won by 238 runs.

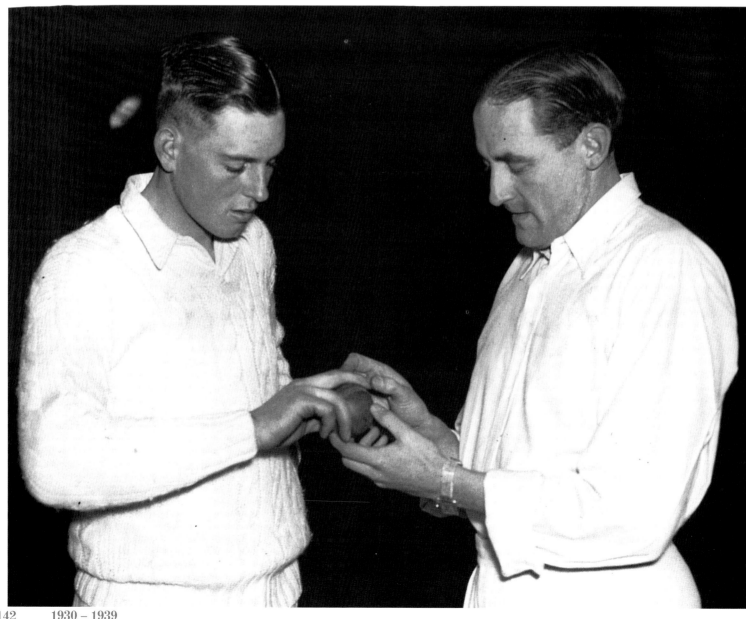

OPPOSITE BOTTOM Mr Jack Nye (left), formerly a farm worker in Sussex, receives instructions from Allen Fairfax, in January of 1934, on the best method of gripping the ball. Nye, a fast bowling discovery at the time was looked upon as a second Larwood. Fairfax was an all-rounder and played 10 Tests for Australia from 1928/29 to 1930/31. He took 21 wickets at 30.71 with a best of 4 for 31 against the West Indies in the fourth Test at Melbourne. And he scored 410 runs at an average of 51.25, with a high score of 65 against England in the Fifth Test of the 1928/29 series at Melbourne.

ABOVE Australia's Grimmett bowling with England's Sutcliffe at the non strikers end. Grimmett finished with 5 for 81 in England's first innings in this opening Test of the 1934 Ashes series in England. Along with his spin bowling partner, Bill O'Reilly combined to destroy England in this match, with Grimmett taking 5/81 and 3/39 and O'Reilly taking 4/75 and 7/54. Australia won the Test by 238 runs.

ABOVE Third day of the Fourth Test between England and Australia in 1934. Australia's Arthur Chipperfield scores off a ball from Bill Bowes.

LEFT The First Test match of the same series was Chipperfield's Test debut. Batting at number 7, he reached 99 by lunch on day two. However, he was dismissed third ball after the resumption still on the same score.

ABOVE E.Holmes (left), captain of a visiting MCC team and Vic Richardson (right), captain of the Australian team for the forthcoming tour to South Africa, having a chat in Perth in 1935.

RIGHT Al Burke, the middleweight champion of Australia presents his old school chum, Arthur Chipperfield, with a signature pair of boxing gloves autographed by every well known boxer in the country in October, 1934. In the centre is Burke's wife.

TOP LEFT On his first appearance in a Sheffield Shield match Don Bradman had scored a century for New South Wales, which was against South Australia. And now in his first appearance for South Australia, he made another, and it was against his old team from New South Wales. South Australia Sheffield Shield team from 1935–36: Left to right, Standing: F.H.Collins, F.A.Ward, T.W.Wall, R.G.Williams, T.R.O'Connell, E.J.R.Moyle, A.F.Richter. Seated: R.A.Parker, C.W.Walker, D.G.Bradman (Captain), A.J.Ryan, M.G.Waite. In Front: R.A.Hamence, C.L.Badcock.

TOP RIGHT Ah ... the old days huddled around the radio ... schoolmates of John Bradman (near radio, fourth from right) cheered with him when his father passed yet another century.

RIGHT England batsman Robert 'Bob' Elliott Storey Wyatt, a determined batsman and handy medium pace bowler played 40 Tests for England from 1927–28 to 1936–37. He scored 1839 runs at an average 31.7, with a high score of 149 against South Africa in the First Test at Trent Bridge in 1935. He also took 18 wickets at 35.66, with a career best of 3/4 against South Africa in 1928. He was appointed captain for England's last Test against the touring Australians in 1930, but lost the role to Douglas Jardine for the next few years. In the 1932/33 tour to Australia, Wyatt

was in charge of an early tour match that Jardine sat out, and therefore became the first captain to employ the Bodyline tactics. After the political and administrative fallout caused by Bodyline, Wyatt was reinstated as captain and led England in a further 15 Tests.

ABOVE W.R.Hammond and Don Bradman walking out to inspect the pitch at Lord's in the Second Test of the 1938 series.

Construction work on the new grandstand at the Sydney Cricket Ground in August 1935. When completed it would be named the MA Noble Stand in honour of the great cricketer.

ABOVE Bill Voce, the English fast bowler sends down a delivery in the 1936/37 Ashes series in Australia, while Australian opening batsman Bill Brown backs up at the non-strikers end. Voce was England's leading wicket taker in this series, taking 26 wickets at 21.53. In England's wins in the first two Tests of that series Voce was brilliant, capturing 6/41 and 4/16 in the First Test at Brisbane and 4/10 and 3/66 in the Second Test at Sydney. Bill Brown played for Australia in 22 Tests from 1932–33 to 1949–50, scoring 1592 runs at an average of 46.82, with a high score of 206.

LEFT The 1936 Australia team, which was the first Australia team captained by the great Don Bradman. In this series the Australians lost the first two Tests, but came back and captured the final three, for a thrilling series win. Left to right, Back Row: C.L.Badcock (inset), A.G.Chipperfield, E.L.McCormick, M.W.Sievers, W.J.O'Reilly, F.A.Ward. Seated: R.G.Gregory, L.P.J.O'Brien, S.J.McCabe, D.G.Bradman (Captain), J.H.Fingleton, W.A.Oldfield.

ABOVE Members of the All-India cricket team at practice at Alan Fairfax's cricket school at Thames House, Millbank, London. The photo shows Jack Hobbs, the famous Surrey and England cricketer displaying an autographed cricket bat to N.J.Copalan, L.P.Jai and the Mabarajiaunar of Visianagram (captain) in April, 1936.

RIGHT Englishmen G.O.Allen and G.Duckworth aboard the ship the SS Orontes on their way to Australia for the 1932–33 tour.

OPPOSITE TOP LEFT Laurence John Nash, was a Tasmanian who appeared in just two Test matches for Australia, against South Africa in 1931–32 and England 1936–37. A right-arm fast bowler, powerfully built, he took 4/18 and 1/4 in the Fifth Test at Melbourne. His only other Test was against G.O.Allen's England tourists of 1936–37 in the deciding Fifth Test, taking 4/70 in the first innings.

OPPOSITE TOP MIDDLE J.Hardstaff, who top-scored for England in the Fifth Test of the 1936–37 Ashes series, with a first innings total of 83. Match Scores: Australia 604 (D.G.Bradman 169, C.L.Badcock 118, S.J.McCabe 112, R.G.Gregory 80, K.Farnes 6 for 96); England 239 (J.Harstaff 83, T.S.Worthington 44, W.J.O'Reilly 5 for 51, L.J.Nash 4 for 70) and 165 (W.R.Hammond 56, C.J.Barnett 41). Australia won by an innings and 200 runs.

OPPOSITE TOP RIGHT Richardson (left) and McCabe, captain and vice-captain of the Australian cricket team in South Africa, smile their appreciation of a floral tribute at one of the many functions attended by the team in the 1935–36 tour.

OPPOSITE BOTTOM The Fifth Test at The Oval in August, 1934. Allen attempts to pull a ball from W.J.O'Reilly to leg, but is out for a quick fire 19. Match Scores: Australia 701 (W.H.Ponsford 266, D.G.Bradman 244, W.M.Woodfull 49, W.A.S.Oldfield 42, W.E.Bowes 4 for 164. G.O.B.Allen 4 for 170) and 327 (D.G.Bradman 77, S.J.McCabe 70, H.I.Ebeling 41, W.E.Bowes 5 for 55, E.W.Clark 5 for 98); England 321 (M.Leyland 110, C.F.Walters 64) and 145 (W.R.Hammond 43, C.V.Grimmett 5 for 64). Australia won by 562 runs.

ABOVE Len Darling superbly catches Hammond for 32 on a rain-affected Melbourne wicket in the Third Test of the 1936-37 series. Match Scores: Australia 200 for 9 dec (S.J.McCabe 63) and 564 (D.G.Bradman 270, J.H.W.Fingleton 136, K.E.Rigg 47); England 76 for 9 dec (M.W.S.Sievers 5 for 21) and 323 (M.Leyland 111, R.W.V.Robins 61, W.R.Hammond 51, L.O.B.Fleetwood-Smith 5 for 124). Australia won by 365 runs.

ABOVE A hatless Victor Richardson leads out his team on to the field for the First Test at Durban in 1935-36, a series Australia won 4-1. Match Scores: South Africa 248 (E.A.B.Rowan 66, L.O'B.Fleetwood-Smith 4 for 64) and 22 (A.D.Nourse 91, I.J.Siedle 59, W.J.O'Reilly 5 for 49); Australia 429 (S.J.McCabe 149, A.G.Chipperfield 109, W.A.Brown 66, L.S.Darling 60, A.B.C.Langton 4 doe 113) and 102 for 1(W.A.Brown 55). Australia won by 9 wickets.

LEFT Clarrie Grimmett looking down on his shattered stumps, bowled by Sims for 33, playing for South Australia against the English tourists of 1936–37.

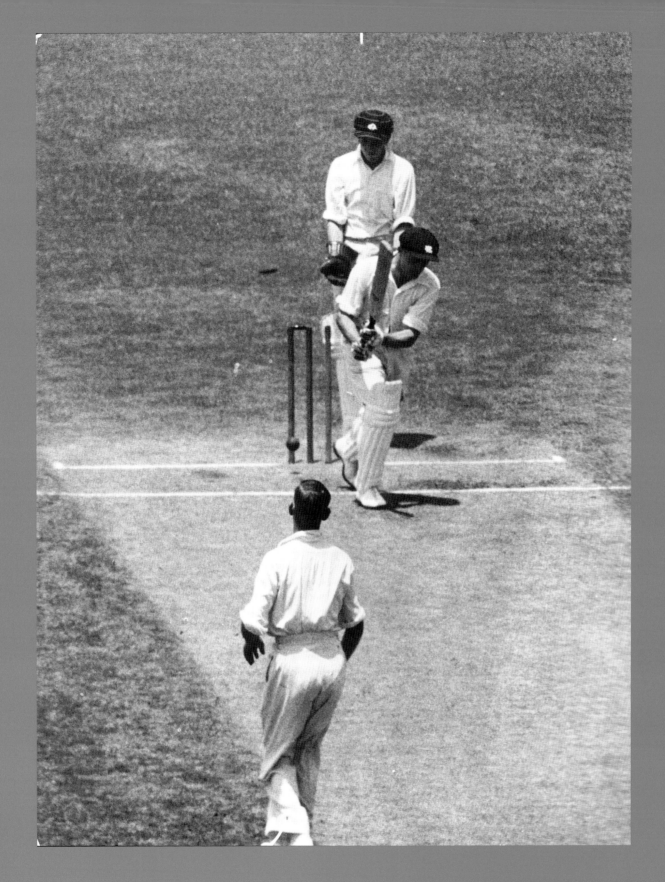

Victorian Len Darling is dismissed for 111 at the Melbourne Cricket Ground by Queensland's Cook. This was an innings that helped secure his Test recall for the Third Test of 1936/37, after Australia were thrashed by an innings and 22 runs in the Second Test in Sydney.

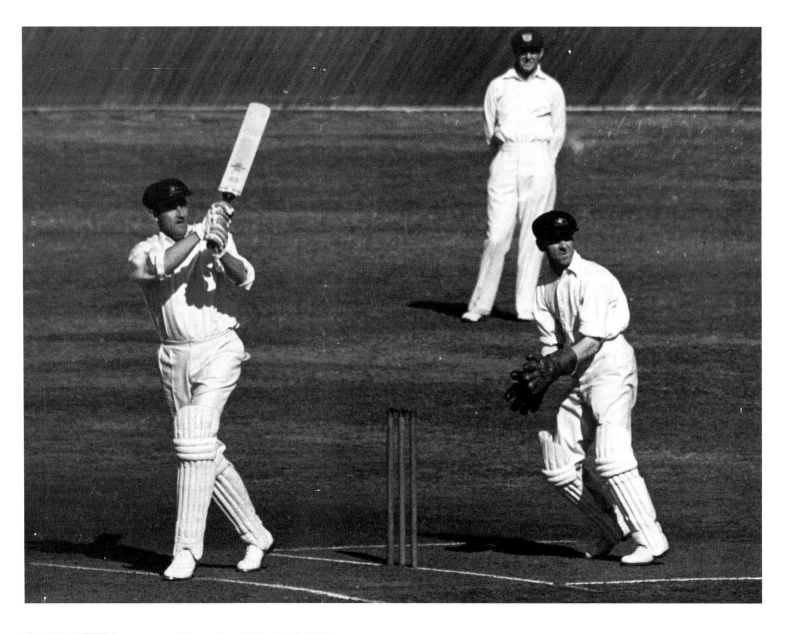

ABOVE Alan Fairfax scores a boundary on the leg side in the Bardsley Fund Cricket Match at Pratten Park, September 1936.

LEFT Warren Bardsley, in his role as New South Wales selector, looks on from the stand during the Country Week Cricket Carnival in the mid 1930s.

Australian spin-bowler, Clarrie Grimmett disembarks after another tour abroad.

ABOVE Ben Barnett, the Hawthorn-East Melbourne and Test wickeeper, practices before the start of a District Firsts match against Richmond at Glenferrie Oval in Melbourne in February, 1938. The popular wicketkeeper and useful left-hand batsman of the late 1930s, had a very long career as a player and administrator. He was deputy to W.A.Oldfield on the 1934 tour to England and South Africa in 1935–36. He succeeded Oldfield after his retirement on the 1938 English tour. While his Test career was brief, with just four Test appearances, he 173 first-class matches from 1929–30 through to 1961! He was also a prisoner of war at Changi for several years during the war. He also had a long association with his district club in Melbourne, which had continued until his death in 1979.

LEFT AND OPPOSITE BOTTOM Arthur Gordon Chipperfield, who played 14 Tests for Australia from 1934 to 1938. He scored 552 runs at an average of 32.47, with a high score of 109 against South Africa in the First Test at Durban. He was also a leg-break bowler, who took just 5 wickets, with a best return of 3 for 91. He was selected for the 1934 team to tour England after just three first-class innings for New South Wales.

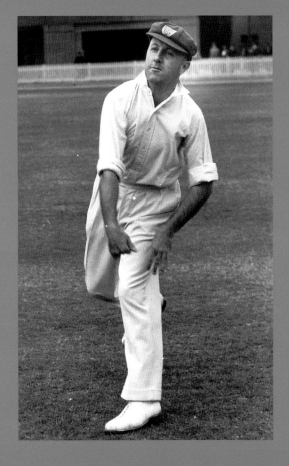

ABOVE Don Bradman shaking hands with King George VI at Lord's, London, during the Second Test, when the Australian team members were introduced to His Majesty during the tea interval. Left to right: S.J.McCabe, B.A.Barnett, J.Fingleton, E.L.McCormick, L.O.B.Fleetwood-Smith, W.J.O'Reilly, W.A.Brown, A.G.Chipperfield

He was selected for the 1934 team to tour England after just three first-class innings for New South Wales

ABOVE A composite photo of both the Australian and English teams taken during the Second Test at Lord's in 1938. Match Scores: England 494 (W.R.Hammond 240, E.Paynter 99, L.E.G.Ames 83, W.J.O'Reilly 4 for 93, E.L.McCormick 4 for 101) and 242 for 8 dec (D.C.S.Compton 76, E.Paynter 43); Australia 422 (W.A.Brown 206, A.L.Hassett 56, W.J.O'Reilly 42, H.Verity 4 for 103) and 204 for 6 (D.G.Bradman 102, A.L.Hassett 42). Match drawn.

BELOW The 1938 Australian touring team. Left to right, standing: W.H.Jeanes (Manager), S.G.Barnes, E.L.McCormick, W.J.O'Reilly, E.S.White, L.O.B.Fleetwood-Smith, J.H.Fingleton, W.Ferguson (Scorer). Seated: W.A.Brown, A.G.Chipperfield, S.J.McCabe, D.G.Bradman (Captain), B.A.Barnett, M.G.Waite, F.A.Ward. In front: C.W.Walker, C.L.Badcock, A.L.Hassett

ABOVE Openers Len Hutton and Maurice Leyland, who shared a record partnership of 382 in the Fifth Test at The Oval in 1938. Leyland was run out for 187 while Hutton was eventually dismissed by O'Reilly for a new then world record of 364, in England's total of 903 for 7. England eventually won the match by an innings and 579 runs.

LEFT Paynter (England) hits a six into the crowd off Fleetwood-Smith (Australia) in the Second Test at Lord's in 1938. He scored 99 and 43 in this match. Match Scores: England 494 (W.R.Hammond 240, E.Paynter 99, L.E.G.Ames 83, W.J.O'Reilly 4 for 93, E.L.McCormick 4 for 101) and 242 for 8 dec (D.C.S.Compton 76, E.Paynter 43); Australia 422 (W.A.Brown 206, A.L.Hassett 56, W.J.O'Reilly 42, H.Verity 4 for 103) and 204 for 6 (D.G.Bradman 102, A.L.Hassett 42). Match drawn.

BELOW Second Test match at Lord's between England and Australia in 1938. England's number three, Edrich is clean bowled by E.L.McCormick for a duck in the first innings. McCormick took the wickets of the top four English batsmen in this innings: Hutton, Barnett, Edrich and Hammmond and finished with 4 for 101.

RIGHT Fingleton (Australia) cuts one through slips off Watts against Surrey at the Oval in 1938

BELOW Jack Fingleton and Don Bradman walking along The Strand in London with an escort of admiring youngsters being kept in tow by a 'Bobby' in 1938.

BELOW RIGHT A fine stroke by Badcock, pulling a ball from F.B.Brown to the boundary during his innings for Australia against Surrey at the Oval in 1938.

LEFT AND ABOVE John Henry Webb Fingleton (Jack), a right-handed opening batsman played 18 Tests for Australia from 1931/32 to 1938, scoring 1189 runs at an average of 42.46, with a high score of 136 against England in the Third Test at Melbourne. A journalist, he joined the Army at the outbreak of the Second World War, before being hired as Press Secretary to the Pime Minister of the day. During the Third Test of the Bodyline series in 1932/33, Fingleton was, some say unfairly, blamed for leaking details of the Australia dressing-room exchange between Australia's captain Bill Woodfull and England's manager Plum Warner, and almost led to the abandonment of the remainder of the Test series. To make this game a complete disaster for Fingleton, he was also dismissed for a pair. After his retirement he was for 34 years the political correspondent for Radio Australia. One of his closest friends during this time was Sir Robert Menzies.

RIGHT Australian cricketer Bill Brown demonstrating a machine gun's capabilities to recruits, with Major General Cameron, Lt Col Grant and with military brass looking on. During the Second World War, Brown was on active duty in the Pacific as a lieutenant.

Fingleton was, some say unfairly, blamed for leaking details of the Australia dressing-room exchange between Australia's captain Bill Woodfull and England's manager Plum Warner

TOP Keith Miller and Cec Pepper head out to bat in one of the Victory Tests, in Yorkshire in September, 1945.

BOTTOM The two captains, W.R.Hammond (England) and A.L.Hassett (Australia) chat before the same game.

1940 – 1949

4

1940

WITH INTERNATIONAL CRICKET ABANDONED DURING WORLD WAR TWO, Australia competed in only 17 Tests in the later half of the 1940s. While most were against England there was also the maiden Test match against New Zealand (1946), a ground-breaking tour by India (1947–48) and a visit by South Africa in 1 949–50. Australia remained undefeated during this period, winning 13 Tests and drawing the other four. Despite approaching forty years of age, Donald Bradman was again the stand-out Australian player.

Australia remained undefeated during this period, winning 13 Tests and drawing the other four.

On Sunday 3 September 1939, Australian Prime Minister Robert Menzies followed England's lead in declaring war on Germany but urged Australians to 'carry on with their normal duties.' The world of cricket attempted to comply with Menzies' plea. As Australia entered the New Year with some uncertainty, NSW won the last Sheffield Shield competition decided for the duration of the conflict. NSW defeated Victoria by 177 runs in the final (despite centuries in each innings by Victorian Lindsay Hassett) but again, the talking point was the form of Don Bradman whilst playing for South Australia. Bradman scored 1475 runs at an average of 122.7 (with a top score 267 against Victoria) during the 1939-40 Shield season.

In March 1940 a match between Sheffield Shield winners NSW and 'The Rest' was programmed for the SCG. A NSW team including Mort Cohen, Stan McCabe and Sid Barnes won the match by two wickets after the home team trailed 'The Rest' on the first innings. Lindsay Hassett scored 136 for 'The Rest', Bill Brown knocked out a classy 97 and veteran bowler Clarrie Grimmet captured 5/65. Don Bradman contributed 25 and 2 but his attention, like the rest of the nation, may have been on other matters. Soon after, the greatest batsmen of his generation — age 32 and in the prime of his career — enlisted in the RAAF. Unfortunately, a crippling illness prevented him from serving his country and he later transferred to the Army School of Physical and Recreational Training where he acted as a trainer.

It would be another five years before the world returned to some resemblance of normality and international cricket resumed its proud history.

During World War II (1939–45), the game of cricket was still played by Australian teams in the far corners of the world. An AIF team won three matches in Egypt in October 1941 against an Alexandria XI, a New Zealand Base XI and the Gezira Sporting Club. Lindsay Hassett scored two centuries in the series. In June 1943 the RAAF cricket team played a charity match against an England team selected by 'Bodyline' tour manager 'Plum' Warner at Lords. Keith Carmody, Stan Sismey and Keith Miller played for the RAAF while the England team included Bob Wyatt, 'Gubby' Allen, Dennis Compton, Trevor Bailey and Alec and Eric Bedser. England won the match but 24-year-old RAAF Sergeant Pilot Keith Miller won the admiration of the local fans with a fighting century amid the threat of two V1 bombs that exploded nearby. The following July, the RAAF played a West Indies team captained by Learie Constantine at Edgbaston. The Army Entertainment Group included first class cricketers such as Stan McCabe, Bill Alley, Bill O'Reilly, Sid Barnes, Don Tallon, Clarrie Grimmet, Colin McCool and Ron Saggers among others — the nucleus of a competitive Test team!

In May 1945, a combined Services team was formed with Lindsay Hassett as captain and took on England at Lords in the first of five 'Victory Tests' during the final summer of the war. By August, with the War in the Pacific also won, over 367,000 people had watched the five Test series in England. Despite only having one Test player in their ranks (Hassett) the Australian Services team won the first 'Test' by six wickets after Miller scored 105 in the first innings. England won the second match at Sheffield before the Australian won the third, at Lords, by 4 wickets. The fourth 'Test' of the series, which saw Miller score another century at Lords, was drawn but England squared the ledger in the fifth match at Old Trafford with a 6 wicket victory. In October, the Australian Services team commenced a six week tour of India and played three 'Tests' against an Indian representative team before finishing — somewhat exhausted — with a six-state tour of Australia over the summer of 1945–46.

the first post-war Test match was played against New Zealand in Wellington on 29 March 1946

On the final day of 1945, Donald Bradman made 112 for South Australia against the Australian Services team at Adelaide.

The Australian Board of Control met for the first time after the end of the war on October 11 1945 and immediately issued an invitation to England to conduct a tour of Australia in the summer of 1946–47. However, the first post-war Test match was played against New Zealand in Wellington on 29 March 1946. After travelling across the Tasman on cricket tours during the past 75 years, this was the first cricket Test played between the two nations. The match had first been earmarked for 1940, but five years after an inaugural 'Trans-Tasman Test' were abandoned because of the war, New Zealand showed that they were barely up to international standard when they were beaten by Australia in two days. In fairness, several prominent first class Kiwi players had not returned from the War, but after the heavy loss the New Zealanders would carry an 'antipodean' inferiority complex for decades to come.

Bill Brown captained Australia against New Zealand in the one-off Test in the absence of Don Bradman, who was recovering from illness and injury. The Kiwis were led by Captain Walter Hadlee, the father of three sons who would also play cricket for their country —

1949

1940

Dayle, Barry and Sir Richard Hadlee. The New Zealand captain won the toss and elected to bat on a damp pitch but the Kiwis were dismissed for just 42 runs in the first innings. 40 year-old Bill O'Reilly took 5/14, Ernie Toshack 4/12 and former St George rugby league winger Ray Lindwall captured his first Test wicket. Australia declared at 8/199, with Bill Brown top-scoring with 67, and then bowled New Zealand out for 54 to win by an innings and 103 runs. 'Tiger' O'Reilly announced his retirement after capturing 8/33 in the Test.

In 1946-47 England, captained by Wally Hammond, returned to Australia after an absence of ten years. Don Bradman, still recovering from surgery for a debilitating illness, agreed to captain Australia even though he had not picked up a bat during the year. In the first Test in Brisbane, Bradman scored 187 — after being 'caught' on a bump ball at 28 — in Australia's first innings total of 645 (Lindsay Hassett scored 128). England crumbled to be all out for 141 and after following-on, ultimately lost the first Ashes Test by an innings and 332 runs. Australia won the second Test in Sydney by an innings and 33 runs (Sid Barnes scored 234) with the drawn Test in Melbourne meaning that the Ashes would remain with the Australians. After another draw in Adelaide, with centuries to Arthur Morris (122) and Keith Miller (141) Australia finished a 3–0 series win with a 5 wicket victory in Sydney. Bradman praised the quick resumption of Test cricket so soon after the war but was quoted as saying that it was 'unlikely' that he would travel to England to defend the Ashes in 1948.

Australia was two-up in the series and was being heralded as the finest squad ever to leave these shores

In October 1947, the first Indian team visited Australia. Fifteen years after an historic tour of England - and eleven years after the Maharajah of Patiala sponsored a tour of India by an unofficial Indian team — Lala Armanath led India in the first five-Test series against Australia. In the first Test played between the two countries, Australia scored 8 declared for 382 (Bradman was out for 185, hit wicket of all things) before bowling India out for 58 and 98 to record an innings and 226 run victory in Brisbane. The second Test of the series was drawn but Australia completed a 4-0 landslide with a 233 run, an innings and 16 run, and lastly an innings and 177 run wins in the next three Tests. In the Third Test in Melbourne, Bradman scored centuries in both innings and followed this with a double century in Adelaide (overshadowing, but only just, Lindsay Hassett's 198). Teenager Neil Harvey top-scored in the fifth Test in Melbourne, with 153. The best of the Indian batsmen, M.H. 'Vinoo' Mankad (centuries in the third and fifth Tests) caused a furore when he ran out Australian batsman Bill Brown at the non striker's end without warning in the second Test. Mahkad was pilloried in the Australian press for dislodging the bails when Brown walked out of the crease to back up the batsman, but Bradman later defended the move by simply saying that the laws of cricket were 'quite clear' on the matter.

The 'Mankad' dismissal quickly became part of the game's vernacular.

The 1948 Ashes series, acknowledged as Don Bradman's farewell to cricket, was the cause of enormous expectation. The 17-man Australian squad arrived in England in April with only four members having toured England before (Bradman, Barnes, Hassett and Brown) while Miller had shown great form in the 'Victory Tests'. By the end of June, Australia was two-up in the series and was being heralded as the finest squad ever to leave these shores. Bradman opened the series with 138 in the first innings of Australia's 8 wicket victory at Nottingham. The visitors then won the second Test, at Lords, by 409 runs to take a stranglehold on the Ashes trophy. When the third Test was drawn, the Ashes were retained but Australia showed its complete dominance with victories in the remaining Tests of the series.

In the fourth Test at Leeds Australia became the first team to score over 400 in the second innings to win a Test match. Set 404 for victory on the final day of play, Morris scored 182 and Bradman 173 not out to record a famous victory. In the final Test of the series at The Oval in London, Bradman needed only four runs to take his Test career average to 100. After bowling England out for just 52, with Ray Lindwall taking 6/20, it appeared Australia would only need one innings for victory. Openers Barnes and Morris quickly sped past England's first innings score and when Bradman finally came to the crease late on the first day, the capacity crowd gave the Australian captain a huge ovation. Taking his position, rival captain Norman Yardley called upon the crowd to give 'The Don' three loud cheers. Bradman was moved by the reception — even taking his time to take up his stance. Leg spinner Eric Hollies had Bradman stepping back and playing defensively. The second ball — a full length 'wrong'un' — rattled the stumps.

Don Bradman was mortal after all — bowled for 0 in his final Test

Don Bradman was mortal after all — bowled for 0 in his final Test innings. Maybe the Australian captain had not seen the ball because of the mist in his eyes … just maybe. Morris went on to score 196 and Australia — 'The Invincibles of 1948' won the match by an innings and 149 runs to keep their unbeaten record on tour intact. But all we remember today is Bradman's duck.

Don Bradman, who celebrated his 40th on August 27 at Lords with a score of 150 against a 'Gentleman's X1' was honoured with a knighthood in the New Years honours list for services to cricket. The Australian domestic season in 1948–49 saw a series of farewell matches and testimonials for Bradman (Melbourne) and retired players from the beginning of his career such as Arthur Richardson (Adelaide) and Bert Oldfield and Alan Kippax (Sydney). On March 15, Sir Donald Bradman was knighted by the Australian Governor General, Sir William McKell at a ceremony at Government House.

As the most turbulent decade known to mankind drew to a close, Australia undertook a tour of South Africa in the summer of 1949–50. Lindsay Hassett was the logical choice as Bradman's successor to the Australian Test captaincy, but he only got the nod from the Australian Board of Control (of which Bradman was now a member) by a single vote. In the final week of December, a century by Hassett guided Australia to an innings and 85 runs win over South Africa in Johannesburg.

1949

The 1940s was very much the end of an era in Australian cricket.

OPPOSITE PAGE Two Australian greats, Bert Oldfield and Arthur Mailey, meet again at a cricket match during the 1940s. Mailey, a journalist of the day and Oldfield, a sports store proprietor and keen spectator.

RIGHT Montague Alfred Noble, who during his long career demonstrated excellent ability in every facet of the game. He was a brilliant batsman, bowler, fieldsman and captain. In 39 Test matches against England he scored 1905 runs at 30.72 and captured 115 wickets at 24.78. His best bowling performance against England was in the Second Test in Melbourne in 1902, when he captured 7/17 and 6/60. When he retired in 1920, he had scored 14245 runs and taken 654 wickets in first-class cricket spanning 28 years from 1893–94 through to 1919–20.

BELOW Herbert Collins, veteran cricketer played 19 Tests for Australia from 1920/21 to 1926, scoring 1,352 runs at an average of 45.06, with a high score of 203 against South Africa in 1921/22 in the Second Test at Johannesburg. He also captained the AIF team in England in 1919, after the First World War. A bookmaker by profession, his nickname was 'Horseshoe' because of his luck in racing and good fortune in winning the toss at cricket. He captained Australia in 11 Tests, including the 1926 side to England. A batsman with sound defence and unlimited patience, he batted for 4 hrs and 50 mins for 40 runs in the fourth Test at Old Trafford in 1921, when Australia's only chance was to bat out for a draw.

ABOVE Sid Barnes, wearing his New South Wales cap, warms up in the nets prior to the Second Test in Sydney in 1946 against England.

RIGHT TOP Ian Johnson, Keith Miller and Lindsay Hassett are seen travelling from Brisbane to Sydney for the Second Test against England in 1946. In the First Test in Brisbane, which Australia had won by an innings and 332 runs, Hassett had scored 128 runs and Miller had scored 79 in their teams first innings of 645. Keith Miller then destroyed the English batting in their first innings, taking 7 for 60 runs.

RIGHT BOTTOM When Victorian members of Australia's 1946 First Test team arrived home from Adelaide, from Sheffield Shield duties, they were measured for Australian blazers in an office on Spencer-street station. Here Keith Miller has the tape run over him while Lindsay Hassett waits.

ABOVE Sid Barnes, Australian opening bat turns a ball to leg. Peter Smith (foreground) and Norman Yardley (arms out-stretched) watch its flight. Barnes scored 234 runs in this innings and put on a record 405 with Bradman for the sixth wicket. Bradman had batted down the order because of injury. Match Scores: England 255 (W.J.Edrich 71, J.T.Ikin 60, I.W.Johnson 6 for 42) and 371 (W.D.Edrich 119, D.C.S.Compton 54, C.Washbrook 41, C.L.McCool 5 for 109); Australia 659 for 8 dec (S.G.Barnes 234, D.G.Bradman 234, K.R.Miller 40). Australia won by an innings and 33 runs.

LEFT Queensland captain Don Tallon being congratulated by cricketing friends after his appointment as wicketkeeper in the First Test of 1946/47.

BOTTOM LEFT Sid Barnes (left) and Ian Johnson going out to resume their batting on the second day in the Second Test match of 1946. Johnson had not scored and Barnes was 21 when stumps were drawn on Day 1. Johnson would be dismissed the following day for just seven, while Barnes would go on to his highest Test score in his career.

BOTTOM RIGHT A rare shot of wicketkeeper Don Tallon at bowling practice for the Third Test at the MCG in 1946, a match where he scored 92 with the bat.

Len Hutton flanks English captain Wally Hammond at a press conference on board ship as England arrives in Australia for the 1946/47 tour. Former Australian cricketer and then journalist Jack Fingleton stands alongside Hammond.

Keith 'Nugget' Miller in 1946. He played 55 Tests for Australia from 1945/46 to 1956/57, scored 2958 runs at an average of 36.97, with a top score of 147 against the West Indies in the First Test at Kingston on the 1954/55 tour. He also took 170 wickets at 22.97, with best figures in an innings of 7/60, which was achieved in the First Test of the 1946/47 series at Brisbane. Statistics alone do not do justice to this truly great cricketer. After the misery of World War Two, he enlivened the postwar period with either brilliant strokeplay or a fiery spell of pace bowling. A fighter pilot during the war, he was well aware of the importance of life, and there was more to life than cricket. He was the embodiment of youth, the athletic 'Aussie', a man men admired and women adored. After his retirement he remained in the public eye, he was a journalist and columnist, and was happiest at the cricket or at the races, often seen in deep discussion.

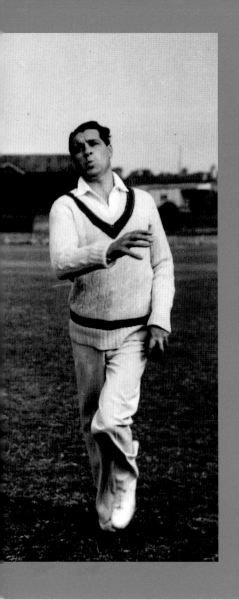

Keith Miller dominated many Test matches, be it in batting, bowling, or fielding, he just loved the game

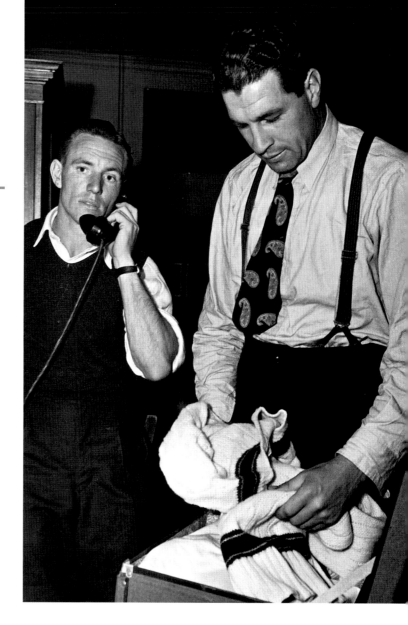

OPPOSITE TOP Australia's left arm medium-pacer Ernie Toshack shows his run up to the wicket and his delivery action, in May 1946. He was one of the games real characters, tall, with striking rugged features, whose good sense of humour was always appreciated by his team-mates. In later years, visitors were always welcome to his home with a drink, good laughs and to reminisce through his scrapbook. Toshack played 12 Tests for Australia from 1945 to 1949/50, taking 47 wickets at an average of 21.04. His best bowling performance was 6/29 against India in the First Test at Brisbane in 1947. Incidentally he took 5/2 in the first innings of that same match, helping dismiss the Indians for 58 and 98.

OPPOSITE BOTTOM Keith Miller twists his foot in the eventful 1948 Test at Manchester. Rain intervened with England on top. This was the only match Bradman's great side may have lost. Match Scores: England 363 (D.C.S.Compton 145, R.R.Lindwall 4 for 99) and 174 for 3 dec (C.Washbrook 85, W.J.Edrich 53); Australia 221 (A.R.Morris 51, A.V.Bedser 4 for 81) and 92 for 1 (A.R.Morris 54). Match drawn.

RIGHT TOP Ernie Toshack packs his bags for the First Test in Brisbane in 1946. His second innings figures of 6 for 82 helped dismiss England for 172, giving Australia a win by an innings and 332 runs.

RIGHT BOTTOM The music-loving punter Keith Miller pulling to the fence in England. Hard to go past as Australia's greatest ever all-rounder, he dominated many Test matches, be it in batting, bowling, or fielding, he just loved the game. For him it was a sport to be enjoyed, and enjoy it he did.

LEFT The classic Keith Miller image, driving past cover. This is how he will always be remembered.

BELOW The Indian Team that toured Australia in 1947/48. Australia won the series 4-0, with one match drawn. Left to right, Standing: W.Ferguson (Scorer), G.Kishenchand, C.R.Rangachari, J.K.Irani, K.M.Rangnekar, K.Rai Singh, P.Sen, K.S.Ranvirsinhji, D.G.Phadkar, H.R.Adhikari, P.Gupta (Manager). Sitting: C.T.Sarwate, Gul Mahomed, S.W.Sohoni, V.S.Hazare (Vice-Captain), L.Amarnath (Captain), V.Mankad, C.S.Nayudu, Amir Elahi.

The Australian X1 that played India in Sydney in November, 1947. The team is, left to right, Back Row: R.Saggers, S.Loxton, B.Dooland, W.Johnston, R.Rogers, M.Herbert. Front Row: K.Miller, R.Hamence, W.A.Brown, D.G.Bradman (Captain), N.Harvey. J.Pettiford. Don Bradman scored his 100th century in this, his 285th innings in first class cricket.

The classic Keith Miller image, driving past cover. This is how he will always be remembered.

ABOVE The Indians were caught on a rain-affected wicket in the First Test in Brisbane in 1947. Match Scores: Australia 382 for 8 dec (D.G.Bradman 185, K.R.Miller 58, A.L.Hassett 48, A.R.Morris 47, L.Amarnath 4 for 84) India 58 (L.Amarnath 22, E.R.H.Toshack 5 for 2, R.R.Lindwall 2 for 11) and 98 (C.T.Sarwate 26, E.R.H.Toshack 6 for 29, R.R.Lindwall 2 for 19). Australia won by an innings and 226 runs.

LEFT Ray Lindwall, one of Australia's greatest ever fast bowlers in action in the Fifth Test at the SCG in 1947. His first innings haul of 7 for 63 tore the heart out of the England line-up.

The Indians were caught on a rain-affected wicket in the First Test in Brisbane in 1947.

RIGHT TOP Len Hutton, who top scored for his team with 122 before retiring ill in the first innings, goes out to bat in the Fifth Test against Australia at the Sydney Cricket Ground in 1947. Match Scores: England 280 (L.Hutton 122, W.J.Edrich 60, R.R.Lindwall 7 for 63) and 186 (D.C.S.Compton 76, C.L.McCool 5 for 44); Australia 253 (S.G.Barnes 71, A.R.Morris 57, D.V.P.Wright 7 for 105) and 214 for 5 (D.G.Bradman 63, A.L.Hassett 47). Australia won by 5 wickets.

RIGHT BOTTOM Lindsay Hassett swinging at a loose ball from Brooks in the Sheffield Shield match between Victoria and New South Wales at Melbourne in December, 1947.

He was a master of the use of the bumper, bowling it sparingly but brilliantly, and the mere possibility of it made batsmen uneasy.

ABOVE Ray Lindwall watches a film of himself bowling. Note the front foot well over the crease, taking good advantage prior to the change to the front foot rule. Starting after the Second World War Lindwall was for a decade without doubt Australia's leading new-ball fast bowler. During the 1930s the game had been dominated by batsmen, with the brief interlude of Bodyline. Lindwall was part of a new era in which bat and ball were more evenly matched. He was a master of the use of the bumper, bowling it sparingly but brilliantly, and the mere possibility of it made batsmen uneasy. Testamount to his greatness was the fact that more than 40 per cent of his 228 test victims were clean bowled. Half way through the home series of 1946/47 against England, both Lindwall and Keith Miller emerged as the undisputed leaders of their countries attack, and the paying public loved them.

ABOVE The 1948 Australians to England. Left to right, Back Row: R.Lindwall, K.R.Miller, W.A.Brown, D.Tallon. Standing: W.Ferguson (Scorer), R.N.Harvey, D.Ring, E.R.H.Toshack, W.A.Johnston, R.A.Saggers, S.G.Barnes, K.O.Johnson (Manager). Seated: S.Loxton, R.A.Hamence, A.L.Hassett, D.G.Bradman (Captain), C.L.McCool, A.R.Morris, I.Johnson.

RIGHT Don Bradman with Captain Allen en route to England aboard the *Strathaird* in 1948. With his enormous abilities, Bradman could have possibly captained the ship as well.

LEFT Don Bradman and his opposing captain toss the coin before the opening match of the 1948 tour of England.

BELOW English captain Norman Yardley (right), greets the Australian captain Don Bradman, at a reception in London prior to the start of the 1948 tour. Mr J.A.Beasley, the Australian High Commissioner, is in the middle.

OPPOSITE Don Bradman leads his team out for the last time, the Fifth Test at the Oval in 1948.
Match Scores: England 52 (R.R.Lindwall 6 for 20) and 188 (L.Hutton 64, W.A.Johnston 4 for 40); Australia 389 (A.R.Morris 196, S.G.Barnes 61, W.E.Hollies 5 for 131). Australia won by an innings and 149 runs.

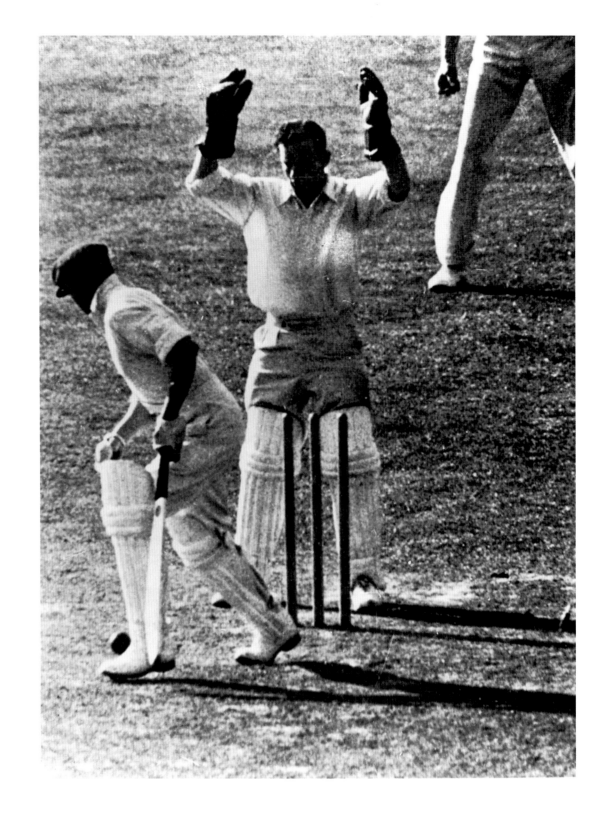

An ironic end to the best batsman
that's played the game.

OPPOSITE Bradman is bowled by Hollies for 0 in his last innings for Australia, the Fifth Test at The Oval in 1948. An ironic end to the best batsman who ever played the game.

ABOVE LEFT Ray Lindwall slashes a four against England. Always a much under-rated batsman, he scored a fine 100 against England in the Fourth Test at Adelaide in the 1946–47 series and 118 against the West Indies in the Fourth Test at Bridgetown in 1955.

ABOVE RIGHT Photo of Warren Bardsley in the 1940s. He was one of Australia's greatest left-handed batsmen. He represented his country in 41 Tests, scoring 2469 runs at 40.47 and played cricket in England, New Zealand, South Africa, Fiji, USA, Canada and Bermuda. The great Englishman Sir Jack Hobbs, said of Bardsley, 'I cannot imagine a nicer fellow.'

LEFT Dudley Nourse, the South African Captain, who took on the Australians in 1949 and commented later, 'Hassett's team was far too good for anything we possess in this country.' Australia won the Test series 4–0, with one drawn.

TOP Don Bradman and the Australian Test cricketers visited Slazengers Showrooms, in London, to collect their equipment at the start of the 1948. The picture shows Don Bradman, inspecting his gloves, watched by Ian Akers-Douglas and E.A.C.Talbot (right).

RIGHT The 1948 Australian cricketers on board the P & O Liner *Strathaird*, during the voyage between Port Said and England in April. Neil Harvey (left) and Sam Loxton are taking part in a game of deck tennis..

OPPOSITE Don Tallon played 21 Tests for Australia from 1946 to 1953. He took 50 catches and 8 stumpings, and scored 394 runs at an average of 17.13, with a high score of 92 against England in the Third Test in Melbourne in 1947. Unusually tall for a wicketkeeper at 5ft 10½in, he was judged by his generation to be the finest keeper. He was alert, agile and sure-handed, his stumpings were subtle, seldom involving the removal of more than one bail. While as a batsman his instincts were attacking, with his highest Test score of 92 made in just 87 minutes.

LEFT The Sheridan Stand at the Sydney Cricket Ground was always a popular place to watch the action from.

ABOVE Touring team mates were interested when Doug Ring, Test slow bowler, received a telegram wishing him the best of luck before the team flew to Tasmania on the first leg of the long trip to England. From left: Bill Johnston, Lindsay Hassett, Ron Hamence, Doug Ring, Sam Loxton, Neil Harvey and Ian Johnson.

The Sheridan Stand at the Sydney Cricket Ground was always a popular place to watch the action from.

ABOVE The sequence of photos show: Sid Barnes faces Trevor Bailey; Barnes decides on hooking, with his right foot moving across quickly; Finally Barnes hooks fast bowler Bailey with a perfect stroke. The match was against Essex at Southend-on-Sea, in one of 12 matches played before the First Test, and boy what a flogging the Australians handed out in this one. Match Scores: Australia 721 (D.G.Bradman 187, W.A.Brown 153, S.J.E.Loxton 120, R.A.Saggers 104); Essex 83 (E.Toshack 5 for 31) and 187 (I.Johnson 6 for 37). Australia won by an innings and 451 runs.

LEFT Australia's Sid Barnes was the second casualty of the Third Test, at Old Trafford, Manchester, when carried off the field after being struck over the kidneys by a drive from Pollard at only five yards range. Throughout the season Barnes had been noted for his daring fielding close to the bat at 'suicide' mid-on. X-Ray examination at Manchester Royal infirmary confirmed that the 30-year-old opening Test batsman had escaped with bruises to the ribs. The first casualty of the Test was Denis Compton, the English batsman, who was struck between the eyes with the ball. Match Scores: England 363 (D.C.S.Compton 145, R.R.Lindwall 4 for 99) and 174 for 3 dec (C.Washbrook 85, W.J.Edrich 53); Australia 221 (A.R.Morris 51, A.V.Bedser 4 for 81) and 92 for 1 (A.R.Morris 54). Match drawn.

RIGHT Wicketkeeper Don Tallon gets padded up for practice at Lord's with the Australian team.

LEFT Arthur Morris and Sid Barnes, who opened in three of the five Tests, posted century stands on two occasions, but on an indivual basis fared even better. Morris finished the tour scoring the most runs and with the best average in the Tests with 696 at an average of 87.0. Barnes also had a great tour, scoring 329 runs at an average of 82.25.

BELOW W.J.Edrich is caught by Tallon after scoring 13 runs in England's second innings at Nottingham in the First Test match. Match Scores: England 165 (J.C.Laker 63, W.A.Johnston 5 for 36) and 441 (D.C.S.Compton 184, L.Hutton 74, T.G.Evans 50, J.Hardstaff 43, K.R.Miller 4 for 125, W.A.Johnston 4 for 147); Australia 509 (D.G.Bradman 138, A.L.Hassett 137, S.G.Barnes 62, R.R.Lindwall 42, J.C.Laker 4 for 138) and 98 for 2 (S.G.Barnes 64). Australia won by 8 wickets.

ABOVE Keith Miller is out, bowled Hollies, stumped Evans for 5 in the Fifth Test. As pleased as he would have been to claim Miller's scalp, Hollies will forever be remembered for dismissing Bradman for a duck in his final Test innings. Match Scores: England 52 (R.R.Lindwall 6 for 20) and 188 (L.Hutton 64, W.A.Johnston 4 for 40); Australia 389 (A.R.Morris 196, S.G.Barnes 61, W.E.Hollies 5 for 131). Australia won by an innings and 149 runs.

BELOW The tour didn't all go Australia's way, as Keith Miller falls well outside his crease after being struck a cruel blow from the wily Alec Bedser during the Third Test at Old Trafford.

RIGHT The Australian touring team opened their tour with a three-day match against Worcestershire. For the English county and Test sides, this was a taste of things to come, with Arthur Morris and Don Bradman reeling off the first of many centuries for the tourists against outclassed opposition. Photo shows D.G.Bradman (left), A.L.Hassett, S.G.Barnes (in background) and E.Toshack (right), going out to start play on the first morning of play.

OPPOSITE BOTTOM Ernie Toshack just manages to scramble back into his crease as McIntyre, the Surrey wicketkeeper, whips off the bails in an attempt to stump him at the Oval. The Surrey X1 had a tough task when they went in to bat after eventually dismissing the Australian touring side for a formidable first innings total of 632. The century makers for Australia on this day were: S.G.Barnes 176, D.G.Bradman 146 and A.L.Hassett 110.

ABOVE Keith Miller makes a spectacular catch to dismiss Hardstaff off Bill Johnston for a duck during the First Test match at Nottingham. Johnston had one of his best ever returns in this innings with 5 for 36 from 25 overs (best was 6 for 44).

OPPOSITE TOP W.J.Edrich is caught by Australian wicketkeeper Tallon, off Lindwall, after making 32 runs during the first day of the Third Test at Old Trafford.

OPPOSITE BOTTOM Australian batsman Sam Loxton is clean bowled by Pollard for 36 during his sides first innings of 221 in reply to England's first innings of 363 in the Third Test at Old Trafford. This Test was England's best chance in the series to this stage of putting Australia under pressure, but they were thwarted by England's inclement weather.

ABOVE LEFT Neil Harvey, the 19-year-old Australian, playing in his first Test match against England, being congratulated by Sam Loxton, after scoring a century on debut, in the Fourth Test at Leeds. To cap the match off for Harvey, he was at the crease when the winning runs were scored in a then world record chase, after England had batted into the last day. Match Scores: England 496 (C.Washbrook 143, W.J.Edrich 111, L.Hutton 81, A.V.Bedser 79) and 365 for 8 dec (D.C.S.Compton 66, C.Washbrook 65, L.Hutton 57, W.J.Edrich 54, W.A.Johnston 4 for 95); Australia 458 (R.N.Harvey 112, S.J.E.Loxton 93, R.R.Lindwall 77, K.R.Miller 58) and 404 for 3 (A.R.Morris 182, D.G.Bradman 173). Australia won by 7 wickets.

ABOVE RIGHT Len Hutton and Cyril Washbrook, the openers for England in the 1948 series against Australia, go out to open the batting. The normally heavy-scoring openers were ineffective against the all-conquering 'Invincbles', led by Miller and Lindwall. Their only innings of any note was the Fourth Test at Leeds, where they put on 168 in the first innings and 129 in the second.

> *The Third Test at Old Trafford was England's best chance in the series to this stage of putting Australia under pressure*

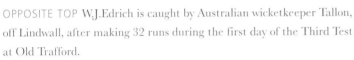

RIGHT Len Hutton who opened the English innings with Cyril Washbrook, hits out at a ball from Lindwall. Hutton scored 81 before being out, in the Fourth Test at Leeds.

BELOW The final Test match at the Oval, shows the Australians go up with delight as J.F.Crapp is caught by Tallon bowled Miller for a duck in England's first innings collapse for 52.

OPPOSITE TOP South Africa's cricket captain, Dudley Nourse (left) greets (left to right) Arthur Morris, Lindsay Hassett and Neil Harvey, of the Australian team on its arrival at Durban on October 7, 1949.

OPPOSITE BOTTOM Australian Test batsman Neil Harvey celebrated his 21st birthday in Durban on October 8, 1949. At a civic reception to the cricketers, Harvey was congratulated by the Mayor of Durban, Mr.L.Boyd.

ABOVE The two teams that took part in the Testimonial Match for A.Kippax and W.Oldfield on February 25 to March 1, 1949. The teams were split into A.R.Morris's X1 v A.L.Hassett's X1. Left to right, Back Row: J.Moroney (M), J.Burke (H), K.Archer (M), G.A.Langley (M), W.Donaldson (12th man), P.Ridings (H). Centre Row: H.Elphinston (Umpire), K.Meuleman (H), F.Johnston (H), K.R.Miller (H), D.Ring (M), W.Johnston (M), R.A.Saggers (H), L.Johnson (M), I.Johnson (M), G.Borwick (Umpire). Front Row: V.N.Raymer (H), A.Walker (H), R.A.Hamence (M), R.N.Harvey (H), A.L.Hassett, A.R.Morris, D.G.Bradman (M), R.R.Lindwall (M), S.Loxton (H).

RIGHT Jack Fingleton, carved a niche in Test cricket when he scored centuries in four consecutive Tests: the last three Tests of South Africa in 1935/36, 112 at Cape Town, 108 at Johannesburg and 118 at Durban, then in the First Test at Brisbane against G.O.Allen's tourists in 1936/37.

Don Bradman walks off the Sydney Cricket Ground after his last innings there in February, 1949. He scored 53 batting for the Morris's X1 against the Hassett's X1.

It's January 1959, a clear sunny day, the Sydney Cricket Ground hill is full, and Australia is playing England in an Ashes battle… is

1950 – 1959

5

1950

AUSTRALIA STARTED THE FIRST 'POST-BRADMAN' DECADE with a five-Test series in South Africa — the first against that nation in fourteen years. Captained by Lindsay Hassett, the Australians sent an SOS for all-rounder Keith Miller after Bill Johnston was involved in a car accident early on tour. Miller, surprisingly left out of the tour by a selection panel headed by Sir Don Bradman, ultimately played in all five Tests. Australia won the series 4–0, with left-hander Neil Harvey's 178 in the Second Test win in Cape Town in the first week of 1950 regarded as the finest knock of the tour. In the Fourth Test in Johannesburg, the only drawn Test of the series, Australian opener Jack Moroney scored a century in each innings (118 and 101 not out) but the tedium of his second innings which frustrated his opposition, the locals and even his team-mates, was completely forgotten by those who witnessed another Neil Harvey ton on the last day of play.

Farcical declarations on a wet Brisbane wicket resulted in England chasing 193 for victory on a 'sticky dog' of a wicket

The legacy built by Bradman's 1948-49 Invincibles is still evident in Australia's authoritative 4–1 series defence of the Ashes in the summer of 1950-51. Farcical declarations on a wet Brisbane wicket in the First Test (England 7/68 declared in response to the home-side's 228, and Australia's 7/32 declared in the second innings) resulted in England chasing 193 for victory on a 'sticky dog' of a wicket. Australian captain Lindsay Hassett's retort to his rival Freddie Brown ('Your move, old chap') as he sent England back in on the fourth day seems today to belong to such a long time ago. England was 6/30 at the end of play before being bowled out for 122 on the final day — 70 runs short of the required total. Test wins in Melbourne, Sydney and Adelaide, where opener Arthur Morris scored 206 in Australia's first innings total of 371, saw Australia retain the Ashes. When England ended the tour with an 8 wicket victory in the final Test of the series, it was their first Test win against Australia since 1938.

In 1951-52 the West Indies returned to Australia after an absence of twenty years. Australia won the first two Tests of the series, by 3 wickets and 7 wickets respectively, but the third Test in Melbourne started in controversy and ended in a sensational West Indian victory. The non-selection of the veteran Sid Barnes had the potential to unsettle the Australian camp but not nearly as much as the Australian Board of Control's handling of the injury to Lindsay Hassett. The Board over-ruled the selectors when they tried to replace the injured Hassett with Phil Ridings (who never did represent Australia) and the Australian captain was forced to act as twelfth man and the team went into the match a batsman short. West Indian medium pacer Frank Worrell took 6/38 and captain John Goddard 3/26 as Australia crumbled to a first innings score of 82. The visitors responded with just 105 but ultimately won the Test by 6 wickets. Australia regrouped to win a tight fourth Test by 1 wicket and finished the five-Test series with a resounding 202 run victory. The series had an

interesting postscript when Sid Barnes, in an effort to have the Board reveal the reasons for his sacking, sued a letter writer to Sydney's *Daily Mirror* who alleged that the veteran batsman was dropped for behaviour of a 'sufficiently serious nature'. The Board's less than impartial reasons for dropping Barnes were tabled in court and were later described by Barnes' counsel as 'tommyrot'.

The following summer Australia hosted a five-Test series against South Africa before heading to England to defend the Ashes. After losing the first Test in Brisbane, the visitors defeated Australia in Melbourne over Christmas which was the first South African Test win against Australia in 42 years. The series ended 2-all but the manner in which the South Africans matched Australia and posted another 6 wicket victory in the fifth Test in Melbourne in February did not bode well for the Ashes tour. In England, the weather influenced the run of drawn results in the first four Tests of the series and heightened tension for a result – any result – in the deciding fifth Test at the Oval. For the first

In the stinging post-mortems after the Ashes defeat, blame was laid squarely at the feet of those men mostly felt to be responsible for the loss

time since the infamous 'Bodyline' series in Australia in 1932, England reclaimed the Ashes by defeating Australia by 8 wickets. England held only a 31 run lead on the third day but bowlers Tony Lock (5/45) and Jim Laker (4/75) dismissed Australia for a paltry 162 amid intermittent rain. When Dennis Compton hit Arthur Morris (of all bowlers!) for four the following day, England celebrated the return of the Ashes as if it were 'VE' Day all over again. In the stinging post-mortems after the Ashes defeat, blame was laid squarely at the feet of those men mostly felt to be responsible for the loss - the members of the Australian Board of Control who were described as 'aloof' and 'out of step' with the cricket-going public.

When Len Hutton's England team returned to Australia to defend the Ashes in 1954-55 all-rounder Ian Johnson, who had been left out of the 1952–53 Ashes tour because of poor form, was the Australian captain. Australia won the first Test in Brisbane by a commanding margin of an innings and 154 runs with centuries to Morris (153) and Neil Harvey (162) but was quickly brought back to earth in the second Test in Sydney. With Morris deputising as captain in the absence of the injured Ian Johnson, England won a tight contest by 38 runs. Utilising a shortened run-up in the harsh Australian conditions, bowler 'Typhoon' Frank Tyson — with match figures of 10/130 in Sydney and 9/95 and 6/132 in the next two Tests — destroyed the home-side's hopes of winning back the Ashes. Australian batsmen failed to score a century in the remainder of the series and England's 5 wicket victory in the fourth Test in Adelaide saw the Ashes return with the England team.

Immediately after the Ashes defeat Ian Johnson led Australia to the West Indies in March 1955. Centuries to Neil Harvey (133) and Keith Miller (147) built the platform for Australia's 9 wicket victory in the first Test and following a drawn result in the second Test, the Australian captain

1959

1950

a team described as 'too old' in some quarters and harshly labelled 'not up to Test standard'

bowled the visitors to victory in the third Test in Georgetown. Johnson took 7/44 in the second innings (after fellow spinner Richie Benaud captured three tail-end wickets in the first innings with four deliveries) with Australian wicketkeeper Gil Langley's five dismissals (three by stumping) equalling the world record set by the great Bert Oldfield in 1924–25. The fourth Test in Bridgetown finished in a draw, with Johnson and Miller clashing heatedly when the Australian captain took the classy all-rounder out of the attack, but the series was stll won. Australia won the fifth Test by an innings and 82 runs with five batsmen — McDonald (127), Harvey (204), Miller (109), Archer (128) and Benaud (121) — scoring centuries in Australia's second innings total of 8 declared for 758.

Australia ventured to England in 1956 with a team described as 'too old' in some quarters and harshly labelled 'not up to Test standard' after the 2–1 series loss. After the first Test at Trent Bridge finished in a draw, Australia took an early lead in the series with a 185 run victory at Lords. But the failure of any Australian batsmen to make a century (Richie Benaud top-scored in the series with 97 in the second Test), the injury to demon bowler Ray Lindwall, the failure to bring back-up spinners and the ages of veteran players Keith Miller, Gil Langley and captain Ian Johnson, were put forward as reasons for Australia's capitulation in the third and fourth Tests. After winning the third Test at Headingly, England spinner Jim Laker mesmerised the Australians on an Old Trafford pitch described as 'a shocker'. Laker took the world record figures of 19/90 in the innings and 170 run victory - including all ten wickets in the Australian second innings — to retain the Ashes. Australia saved face with a draw in the fifth Test but the result did not save the team, or the Board, from far-reaching recriminations and some serious soul-searching after the Ashes defeat.

Following the tour of England, Australia realised a long-term goal of playing a Test series on the sub-continent. Captained by Ian Johnson Australia conducted its first tour of India and Pakistan during the final months of 1956. Pakistan won the first Test played against Australia, in Karachi in October 1956, by 9 wickets with bowler Fazal Mahmood hailed a national hero after capturing 13/114 in the match. Australia were humbled in the first innings — all out for 80 — and responded to Pakistan's 199 with an improved second innings showing of 187, but they still suffered a massive defeat. Australia fared better in India, taking the first Test in Madras by an innings and 5 runs before drawing the second Test under the captaincy of bowler Ray Lindwall. Centuries by Jim Burke (161) and Neil Harvey (140) set up Australia's first innings total of 7 declared for 523 but India ground out a tedious draw. Australia won the final Test of the series at Calcutta, with captain Ian Johnson announcing his retirement after passing the dual milestone of 1000 career runs and 100 Test wickets.

Former teenage batting prodigy Ian Craig captained Australia on the undefeated tour of South Africa in the summer of 1957–58. Not that it was all smooth sailing for the NSW batsman — already Australia's youngest ever Test player at age 17 and 239 days when selected against South Africa in February 1953 — and at age 22, now a Test captain and selector on an overseas tour. Craig was under pressure to 'drop himself' after failures in Australia's first Test draw and then a duck in the innings and 141 run victory in the second Test in Cape Town. But Craig responded with a fighting 52 in the third Test draw before Australia struck form and won the final two Tests of the series. Richie Benaud was the undoubted star of the tour, capturing five wickets in an innings, in four of the five Tests (and passing 100 Test wickets in the process) and scoring a century in the fourth Test in Johannesburg (among four first class centuries that he scored in South Africa and 817 runs amassed). When Ian Craig failed to find form after his premature return from a bout of hepatitis it was Benaud to whom the Board looked as Australia approached the 1958-59 Ashes series.

The Ashes series in the summer of 1958–59 was the first series televised live into Australian households. The ABC paid £5,000 for the rights to show two hours play each day of the first Test in Brisbane. Two commercial channels, ATN 7 in Sydney and GTV 9 in Melbourne, later joined forces to televise the Sydney Test 'live' into Melbourne, which was a first for the fledgling communications medium. Australia set up its Ashes win with 8 wicket victories in each of the first two Tests before the third Test in Sydney finished in a draw. By the time the series moved to Adelaide in February 1959, the talking points revolved around the conservative nature of the England batting, the aggressive captaincy of Richie Benaud and the suspect bowling action of Ian Meckiff. England had queried Meckiff's action in a tour match against Victoria but when the Australian bowler took a match-winning 6/38 in the second Test in Melbourne, tour officials publicly questioned the legality of Meckiff's technique. Meckiff did not play in Adelaide and Australia's authoritative 10 wicket victory to win the Ashes appeared to silence the matter — but as history shows, only temporarily. Veteran bowler Ray Lindwall was recalled for Australia's fifth Test victory in Melbourne and captured a record 216th wicket, and would finish his career with 228 and as Australia's leading wicket taker in 1960.

American President Dwight D. Eisenhower was a less than interested guest in the third Test at Karachi

The decade closed with another tour of Pakistan and India in November-December 1959. Australia won the three-Test series against Pakistan, 2–nil, with American President Dwight D. Eisenhower a less than interested guest in the third Test at Karachi on a day in which Pakistan scored just 104 runs in a day's play. Captained by our own 'king of spin', Richie Benaud, Australia travelled to India in the final weeks of 1959 and although they proved their superiority with a 2–1 series win over the New Year, India won its first Test match against Australia. Playing on a 'matting pitch' provided by the Australian Board of Control in the second Test at Kanpur, Jasubhai Patel took 9/69 in the first innings to set up India's first win in 13 Tests against Australia. Neil Harvey, who started the decade with a century in South Africa, closed the 1950s with a peerless 114 in Australia's first Test win in Delhi.

1959

ABOVE Stan McCabe demonstrates some of the master batsmans techniques to a group of interested country boy hopefuls at the Sydney Cricket Ground No.2. The boys were in Sydney for a week of intensive cricket coaching in January, 1950.

LEFT Everton Weekes scores on this tour were not indicative of his place as one the leading West Indian batsman of all time. Shown here padding up on the Australian tour of the 1951/52 season. Weekes' top scores in that series were 70 in the First Test in Brisbane and 56 in the Second Test in Sydney. The West Indies, captained by Goddard, were soundly beaten 4-1, with Australia's pacemen Miller and Lindwall far too good for the tourists.

ABOVE LEFT Arthur Morris, a left-handed opening bat, at age 18 scored a century in each innings in his initial first-class match in December, 1940, for New South Wales. He debuted for Australia in the 1946/47 Test series against England and made a brilliant start to his career, reeling off three centuries in a row in the second innings of the Third Test (155), then in each innings in the fourth Test (122 and 124 not out). As a member of the 1948 Invincibles tour to England, he scored 696 runs at an average of 87, to be the leading scorer and head the Test averages. In all he played 46 Tests spanning the years 1946 to 1955, scoring 3,533 runs at an average of 46.48, with a high score of 206 against England in the Fourth Test in Adelaide in the 1950/51 series.

ABOVE RIGHT Two great West Indian batsman, Everton Weekes (left) and Frank Worrell (right) leave the field after their fourth wicket stand of 283 against England at Trent Bridge, Nottingham in 1950. West Indies won the Test by an innings and 56 runs and the series 3-1.

ABOVE West Indian great Frank Worrell, a stylish opening or middle-order batsman, was ruthless putting the loose deliveries away.

BELOW A.G.Moyes demonstrates how not to play a stroke to Cook Hill schoolboys, in October 1950. A lover of the game, he was a prominent writer, and also played first-class cricket for South Australia and Victoria. Sadly for Moyes his selection for the tour to South Africa was thwarted when the tour was cancelled because of the outbreak of World War 1. He is now best remembered for his authoritative writing in numerous cricket books, including 'Bradman', published in 1948.

ABOVE Keith Miller and Don Tallon in their juggling act in the First Test against England in December, 1950, after Brown had snicked a chance. Tallon fumbled the ball, which Miller knocked back, but it hit Tallon on the chin and the chance was missed. The two players did however get their revenge, as a short time later Brown was out caught Tallon off the bowling of Miller.

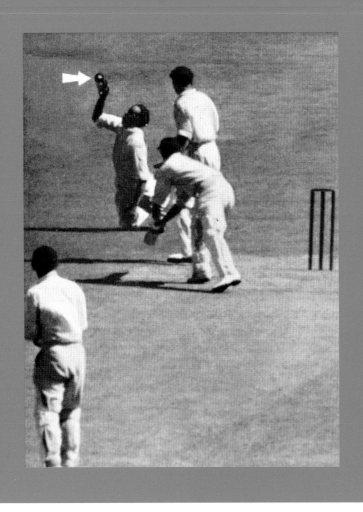
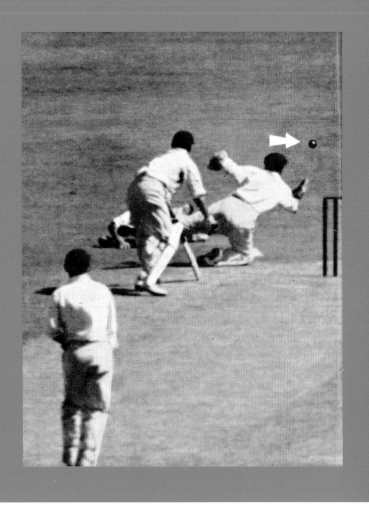

ABOVE One of the most amazing catches in cricket history by the great Queensland wicketkeeper Don Tallon. The first image: England's captain Len Hutton snicks the ball to Ian Johnson at first slip, but Johnson can only deflect the ball. Second image: As the ball flies sideways across the wicket, Tallon starts to dive towards it. Third image: With Hutton watching his downfall, Tallon completes a miraculous catch.

LEFT Don Tallon shows his attacking instincts as a batsman. Although he was without a century in Tests for Australia, averaging only 17.13 in 21 matches, his record was much better in all first-class games. He played 150 in all, scoring over 6,000 runs with 9 centuries and 27 fifties.

RIGHT Lindsay Hassett and Freddie Brown toss at Brisbane prior to the First Test of the 1950/51 Ashes Series. This was a toss that proved eventually crucial in the winning of this game. Hassett won the toss and batted first on a perfect Woolloongabba wicket. Then a downpour later that night followed by bright sunshine had England having to bat on a genuine sticky pitch. Match Scores: Australia 228 (R.N.Harvey 74, R.R.Lindwall 41, A.V.Bedser 4 for 45) and 32 for 7 dec (T.E.Bailey 4 for 22); England 68 for 7 dec (W.A.Johnston 5 for 35) and 122 (L.Hutton 62, J.B.Iverson 4 for 43). Australia won by 70 runs.

Ray Lindwall played in 61 Tests for Australia from 1945/46 to 1959/60, took 228 wickets at 23.03 with a career best 7 for 38 against India in 1948. He was also a very useful batsman, with 1502 runs (which included two centuries) at an average of 21.15, with a high score of 118. Lindwall had renounced rugby union to play cricket after the Second World War. He was Australia's premier new-ball bowler for over a decade, with his powerful, rhythmic run up to the wicket, wonderful control and the ability to get lat swing.

TOP LEFT Sonny Ramadhin, West Indies' spin bowler, was secretive about his bowling grip but he gripped a pen for this photograph and added his name to the other on a souvenir bat at the MCG in November, 1951. With him is Victorian Test bowler Ian Johnson.

TOP RIGHT Test umpires George Borwick (left) and H.Elphinston (right) chat with H.S.Love (who played for Australia in the Bodyline series), who captained the ex-internationals against the West Indies in the Ferguson Testimonial match at North Sydney, in October, 1951.

LEFT Sid Barnes playing Sydney district cricket for Gordon, in October, 1951 emerges from the dressing room with Sid Carroll the other batsman alongside him. Also to play for the famous old club were Test players: Charlie Macartney, Victor Trumper, Charles Kelleway, Bet Oldfield, Neil Harvey, Adam Gilchrist, Frank Iredale and Brian Taber.

ABOVE Ray Lindwall misses a delivery from J.J.Warr, from the Fourth Test at Adelaide Oval in the 1950/51 series. Match Scores: Australia 371 (A.R.Morris 206, K.R.Miller 44, A.L.Hassett 43, R.N.Harvey 43, D.V.P.Wright 4 for 99) and 403 for 8 dec (J.W.Burke 101, K.R.Miller 99, R.N.Harvey 68); England 272 (L.Hutton 156) and 228 (R.T.Simpson 61, L.Hutton 45, D.S.Sheppard 41, W.A.Johnston 4 for 73). Australia won by 274 runs.

LEFT Australia's Test captain Lindsay Hassett inspects the wicket with groundsman Jack Farquhar, after it had been rolled, in Brisbane for the First Test in December 1950. This match was the start of a successful campaign for Hassett's team, winning the series 4–1.

LEFT West Indian Clyde Walcott has been hit by a delivery from Queenslander Raymer, with fellow Queenslander Colin McCool (a 1948 Invincible) checking to see his condition. This was one of the early tour matches in 1951/52.

BELOW The 1951 West Indies cricketers who had been staying in England left aboard the ship the 'Strathamore' before their departure from Tilbury, Essex, to join up with the other members of the team in Australia for the upcomg tour. Left to right, Standing: Roy Marshall, Ken Rickard, Sonny Ramadhin. Seated: Frank Worrell, Clyde Walcott, Ernest Eytle (reporter accompanying the party) and Everton Weekes.

ABOVE LEFT Dudley Nourse, who captained South African when the Australian's visited after the Second World War. Lindasy Hassett's Australian side proved far too good winning the series 4–0. Dudley Nourse headed his countries batting in this series with 405 runs at an average of 45, with a high score of 114 in the Second Test at Cape Town.

ABOVE RIGHT West Indian spin bowling pair Alf Valentine and Sonny Ramadhin in Australia on the 1951/52 tour. Big things were expected from Ramadhin's bowling, but he was not a force on the harder Australian pitches. Valentine however, took 24 Test wickets at an average of 28.

ABOVE LEFT Frank Worrell, played 51 Tests for the West Indies from 1947/48 to 1963, scoring 3,860 runs at an average of 49.48, which included 9 centuries and 22 fifties, and took 69 wickets bowling either left-arm medium pace or slow bowling. An extremely popular player, he first captained his country on the famous 1960/61 tour of Australia. The Frank Worrell Trophy is now played for, between the two countries.

ABOVE RIGHT West Indian, Alf Valentine, the left-handed spinner inspects the ball before taking his turn at the crease. He was the leading wicket-taker for the Windies on the 1951/52 series, with his best figures of 6 for 102 in the Third Test at Adelaide.

Harold Larwood photographed in December, 1952, reading a book on of all subjects, Don Bradman. He emigrated to Australia in 1949, and was working and living in Sydney at this time. Whatever the merits or demerits of the Bodyline controversy, he was one of the greatest fast bowlers in Test cricket. England's captain of the day, Douglas Jardine, devised tactics termed 'leg theory bowling' with Larwood his main strike weapon. England duly won the series 4–1, amid tremendous controversy. He played in 21 Tests from 1926 to 1932/33, taking 78 wickets at an average of 28.35, with a best effort of 6 for 32 against Australia in the First Test at Brisbane in 1928. Was Larwood the real victim of Bodyline, as he would never play Test cricket again after that series?

ABOVE LEFT Old cricketer Herbie Collins in March, 1953, looking dapper in smart snap-brim and snappy bowtie. Interviewed at the time, he said 'the cricket of today isn't as bright as it used to be. Captains are too afraid of losing matches.'

ABOVE RIGHT Australia's Test captain Lindsay Hassett shows West Indies' captain John Goddard how a kangaroos shin bone is used to polish bats, during the 1951/52 season. This was the West Indies first tour to Australia for 21 years.

BELOW The ground staff do their best to cover the wicket as rain interrupts play during England's innings in the First Test at Brisbane in the 1946/47 series. Australia won this match by an innings and 332 runs and the series by 3–0, with 2 draws.

ABOVE LEFT Everton Weekes, who partnered Frank Worrell in some of crickets finest stands since the second world war.

BELOW Everton Weekes caught Langley bowled Lindwall in the Fifth Test at the Sydney Cricket Ground in the 1951/52 Series.

ABOVE RIGHT W.A.Oldfield, one of Australia's greatest ever wicketkeepers, gives some advice to budding cricketers in March, 1952.

ABOVE Edrich hemmed in as England reach out for victory in the Fifth Test at The Oval, 1953. With England within reach of victory and the Ashes, four hostile Australians 'sit on the bat' as W.J.Edrich continues his innings for England. Behind the stumps is wicketkeeper G.Langley, with K.Miller on right and A.Davidson in foreground (back to camera). Match Scores: Australia 275 (R.R.Lindwall 62, A.L.Hassett 53, F.S.Trueman 4 for 86) and 162 (R.G.Archer 49, G.A.R.Lock 5 for 45, J.C.Laker 4 for 75); England 306 (L.Hutton 82, T.E.Bailey 64, R.R.Lindwall 4 for 70) and 132 for 2 (W.J.Edrich 55). England won by 8 wickets.

LEFT Edrich hits a ball from Johnston for four runs, while wicketkeeper Langley looks around in astonishment. Ray Lindwall is at point and Alan Davidson is at short leg.

ABOVE Len Hutton, who top-scored with 82 for England, looks unperturbed dusting his cap which had became dislodged facing Lindwall during the course of play in the Fifth Test against Australia at the Oval in 1953. He was one of the greatest batsman the game has produced. He played in 79 Tests from 1937 to 1955, scored 6,971 runs at an average of 56.67, which included 19 centuries and a top score of 364.

OPPOSITE TOP Fred Trueman, who scored 10 runs, hits a boundary off Johnston on the third day in the Fifth Test at the Oval, in 1953. Match Scores: Australia 275 (R.R.Lindwall 62, A.L.Hassett 53, F.S.Trueman 4 for 86) and 162 (R.G.Archer 49, G.A.R.Lock 5 for 45, J.C.Laker 4 for 75); England 306 (L.Hutton 82, T.E.Bailey 64, R.R.Lindwall 4 for 70) and 132 for 2 (W.J.Edrich 55). England won by 8 wickets.

OPPOSITE BOTTOM Len Hutton bowled by Ray Lindwall before he had opened his score in Yorkshire's first innings against the Australians at Bradford in May, 1953. The county were all out for 145 in reply to Australia's first innings total of 453 for 6 dec.

> *Len Hutton was one of the greatest batsmen the game has produced*

ABOVE England's W.J.Edrich watches the ball trickle past his stumps from a Lindwall delivery in the Fifth Test at the Oval on the 1953 tour. His luck was short-lived as he was out lbw to Lindwall soon after.

BELOW Edrich is given a standing ovation as he comes in after making a fighting innings of 64 in the second innings of the Second Test al Lord's in 1953. Match Scores: Australia 346 (A.L.Hassett 104, A.K.Davidson 76, R.N.Harvey 59, A.V.Bedser 5 for 105, J.h.Wardle 4 for 77) and 368 (K.R.Miller 109, A.R.Morris 89, R.R.Lindwall 50, G.B.Hole 47, F.R.Brown 4 for 82); England 372 (L.Hutton 145, T.W.Graveney 78, D.C.S.Crompton 57, R.R.Lindwall 5 for 66) and 282 for 7 (W.Watson 109, T.E.Bailey 71). Match drawn.

ABOVE Neil Harvey plays a ball to fine leg against Surrey at
The Oval, with wicket-keeper Arthur McIntyre and fieldsman
Alec Bedser trying to stop it.

ABOVE Neil Harvey of Australia is clean bowled by England's Tony Lock in the second innings of the Fifth Test, in 1953. Lock helped England to victory in this match, claiming 5 for 45 in the second innings, which also wrested back the Ashes for the first time in 19 years.

LEFT Sid Barnes batting for New South Wales against South Africa in 1952/53. He was often at odds with the administration and played far less Test cricket than was his due. This was evidenced by the fact that he played just 13 Tests scoring 1072 at an average of 63.05, which included three centuries. He also went on to be an outspoken journalist in the Sydney newspapers.

OPPOSITE BOTTOM Australian and English cricketers on the links at Burnham Beeches, Buckinghamshire, when they met in a golf match in April, 1953. Left to right: England's Jim Laker, Australia's Alan Davidson, former Australian Test cricketer Ben Barnett and Australia's Bill Johnston.

ABOVE The 1953 Australian cricketers, captained by Lindsay Hassett, landed at Southampton from the liner *Orcades*. Lindsay Hassett (left) with Ian Craig, the youngest member of the team at 17. He is the youngest player to ever represent Australia in a Test Match.

LEFT Neil Harvey and Ian Craig going off at lunch in the Fifth Test v South Africa at Melbourne, February, 1953. In Craig's debut for Australia he scored 53 in the first innings and figured in a 148 fourth wicket stand, with Harvey. Harvey went on to reach 205, which was his highest Test score. Interestingly, Craig scored a further 47 in the second innings, thereby scoring exactly 100 in his Test debut.

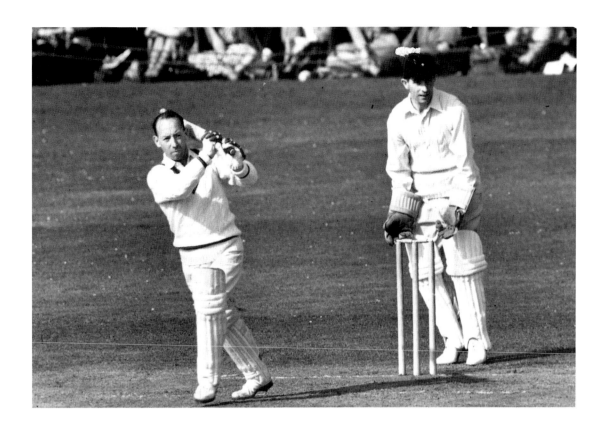

OPPOSITE TOP Ray Lindwall, who top-scored for Australia with 62 in the Fifth Test in 1953, reaches 50 with this shot.

OPPOSITE BOTTOM Ray Lindwall was again scoring heavily down the order in the Second Test, with another 50. Here he slashes one round to leg, while the progress of the ball is watched by England wicketkeeper Godfrey Evans and Captain, Len Hutton.

TOP Lindsay Hassett hitting out at the East Molesey bowling in the Australian's first tour match of 1953.

RIGHT Neil Harvey, after scoring 25 runs for Australia against Cambridge, in May 1953, is caught by wicketkeeper J.Asquith off the bowling of T.Hare.

ABOVE The Duke of Edinburgh, right, seems to be thoroughly enjoying a joke with Australian cricketers, Keith Miller (left) and captain Lindsay Hassett (centre), at East Molesey Memorial Cricket Ground. The 1953 Australians opened their tour with a charity one-day match against the East Molesey team, and the Duke was introduced to the players during the tea interval.

LEFT Friendly conversation between Australian captain Lindsay Hassett (left) and England's captain Len Hutton (right), when the Australian cricket tourists were guests of the British Sportsmen's Club at a Luncheon at the Savoy Hotel, London, in April 1953.

RIGHT Orient liner *Orcades* Ship's Commander, N.A.Whinfield and Australian 1953 cricket team captain, A.L.Hassett pictured at Southampton when the liner arrived with the cricketers. In the background (centre with hat) is Doug Ring (Victorian bowler and batsman), behind Hassett is side-faced Keith Miller (New South Wales), and on the right, in dark raincoat is Ian Craig (New South Wales).

LEFT The opening toss of the tour, at the 'friendly' against East Molesey. Here are the captains, R.J.H.McNeill (left) and A.L.Hassett (right), tossing for choice of innings to start off the game.

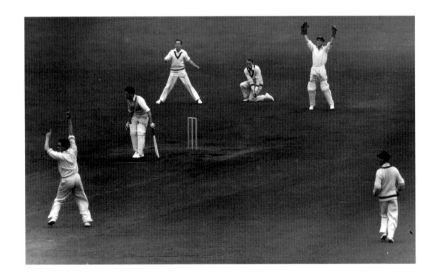

TOP The Fourth Test Match between England and Australia at Leeds ended in a thrilling draw. After a day of high excitement, the match finished with Australia only 30 short with 6 wickets in hand. Photo shows: A.R.Morris (Australia) stumped Evans bowled Laker after scoring a quick 38. Match Scores: England 167 (T.W.Graveney 55, R.R.Lindwall 5 for 54) and 275 (W.J.Edrich 64, D.C.S.Compton 61, J.C.Laker 48, K.R.Miller 4 for 63); Australia 266 (R.N.Harvey 71, G.B.Hole 53, A.V.Bedser 6 for 95) and 147 for 4. Match drawn.

ABOVE The Australians appeal for lbw against Trevor Bailey, England. At top is Australia's wicket-keeper Don Tallon. Surrey and England bowler Alec Bedser took seven second innings Australian wickets in the First Test at Nottingham. This brought his figures for the two innings to 14 for 99. This created a new English Test wicket-taking record, reaching 196, beating the previous best of 189 by Barnes. Match Scores: Australia 249 (A.L.Hassett 115, A.R.Morris 67, K.R.Miller 55, A.V.Bedser 7 for 66) and 123 (A.R.Morris 60, A.V.Bedser 7 for 44); England 144 (L.Hutton 43, R.R.Lindwall 5 for 57) and 120 for 1 (L.Hutton). Match drawn.

ABOVE Len Hutton lived to regret his decision to send Australia in to bat in the First Test of the 1954 Ashes Series. Picture Shows: R.N.Harvey (Australia) swinging A.V.Bedser (England) hard to leg during his first innings century. Match Scores: Australia 601 for 8 dec (R.N.Harvey 162, A.R.Morris 153, R.R.Lindwall 64, G.B.Hole 57, K.R.Miller 49); England 190 (T.E.Bailey 88, M.C.Cowdrey 40) and 257(W.J.Edrich 88, P.B.H.May 44). Australia won by an innings and 154 runs.

LEFT Queensland's first century maker in Shield cricket for the 1954 season was scored by 22-year-old Peter Burge. Here he characteristically hits out by lofting New South Wales spinner Treanor to the mid-wicket boundary at the Gabba. He was eventually out when attempting a big hit off Keith Miller when he was 122.

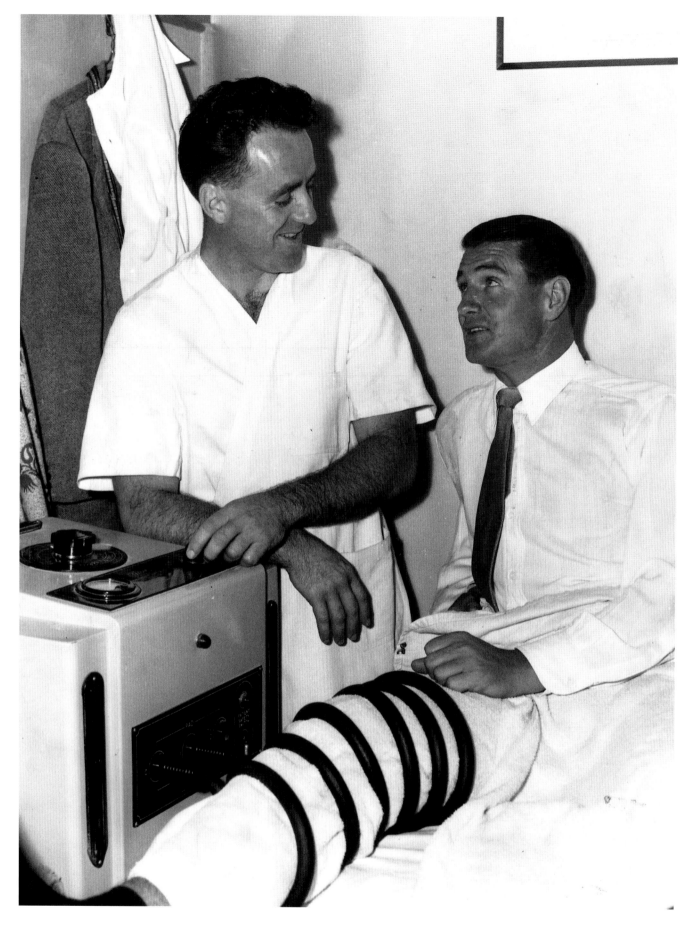

Australian Test star Keith Miller receives ray treatment for his knee injury from masseur Charlie O'Brien. Miller was trying to get fit for the Second Test in 1954 against England at Sydney. Unfortunately for Miller he didn't play and Australia lost the match by 38 runs.

Richie Benaud survives an lbw appeal from England's Brian Statham at Sydney in a tour match in 1954. Looking at the picture you would have to ask, how did he survive?

OPPOSITE TOP A young Richie Benaud looks anxious against England, while playing for New South Wales in November, 1954.

OPPOSITE BOTTOM Benaud lunges at a ball from Bedser in the same game.

BELOW Selectors Dudley Seddon (left), Sir Donald Bradman, and Jack Ryder, watch the Fourth Test between Australia and England at Adelaide Oval in early February, 1955. They were to announce the Australian team for the Fifth Test the following team. This was a Test series which England won 3–1.

ABOVE West Indies Clyde Walcott, the Barbados wicketkeeper and batsman. One of the famous three 'Ws', of Walcott, Weekes and Worrell. Their averages in Tests were: Walcott 56.68 (44 Tests, 3,798 runs); Weekes 58.61 (48 Tests, 4,455 runs) and Worrell 49.98 (51 Tests, 3,860 runs). No wonder they were famous.

LEFT Neil Harvey is caught Evans bowled Statham for 4 in the Australia X1 v MCC in November, 1954.

BELOW Australian captain and opening bat Lindsay Hassett is out leg before wicket with his score at 10 to a ball from England's Jim Laker in their second innings of the Fifth Test of the 1953 series in England.

OPPOSITE TOP The wise, experienced wicket-keeper does not interfere with fieldsmen who have a better chance of catches than he does. Here Len Maddocks makes a borderline decision to try for the catch himself despite the presence of Benaud and Davidson in bowler Ian Johnson's leg trap. The batsman is Colin Cowdrey, his partner is Denis Compton and the series is the 1954/55.

ABOVE Is it a chance? Was it out? Did Colin Cowdrey hit it? Was he leg before wicket? From the intense concentration of umpire Mel McInnes it's certain the answer will be correct. Denis Compton is the other batsman in this 1955 Adelaide Fourth Test photo. Match Scores: Australia 323 (L.V.Maddocks 69, C.C.McDonald 48, K.R.Miller 44, I.W.Johnson 41) and 111: England 341 (L.Hutton 80, M.C.Compton 44, R.Benaud 4 for 120) and 97 for 5. England won by 5 wickets.

OPPOSITE TOP Port of Spain, Trinidad, in the Second Test on April 11, 1955. Jeff Stollmeyer slashes one through slips, with Neil Harvey unable to stop it, in front of a 30,000 strong crowd on day one at picturesque Queen's Park Oval.

OPPOSITE BELOW Clyde Walcott plays defensively at Australia's Lindwall as the Australian's appeal for an lbw decision. Match Scores: West Indies 382 (E.D.Weekes 139, C.L.Walcott 126, R.R.Lindwall 6 for 95) and 273 for 4 (C.L.Walcott 110, E.D.Weekes 87): Australia 600 for 9 dec (R.N.Harvey 133, A.R.Morris 111, C.C.McDonald 110, R.G.Archer 84, I.W.Johnson 66). Match drawn.

TOP Clyde Walcott has a wide grin as he is bowled by Richie Benaud for 83 in the West Indies second innings in the Fourth Test at Bridgetown, Barbados. In the picture are William Watson (fielding), Clyde Walcott (batsman) and Gil Langley (wicketkeeper). The match scores were: Australia 668 and 249; West Indies 510 and 234 for 6. Match drawn.

BELOW Ian Johnson, Australia's skipper, drives straight down the wicket for four, during his aggressive innings of 66 runs on the fifth day of the Second Test against the West Indies.

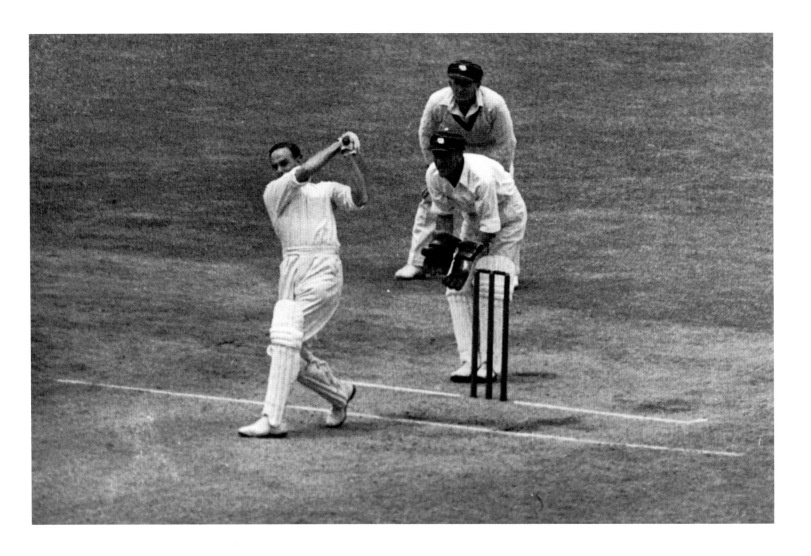

ABOVE Victoria's Ian Johnson, a forceful batsman, is seen here jumping out to on-drive a ball from Queensland's Raymer during the Sheffield Shield game at the MCG in January, 1955.

LEFT Sir Frank Worrell on his first tour to Australia in 1951. The Australian public were captivated by the man, the batsman and on his last tour (1960/61), as captain of one of the most never to be forgotton series ever played.

OPPOSITE Richie Benaud, playing for New South Wales, is caught by Victorian wicketkeeper Len Maddocks for 2 in January, 1955.

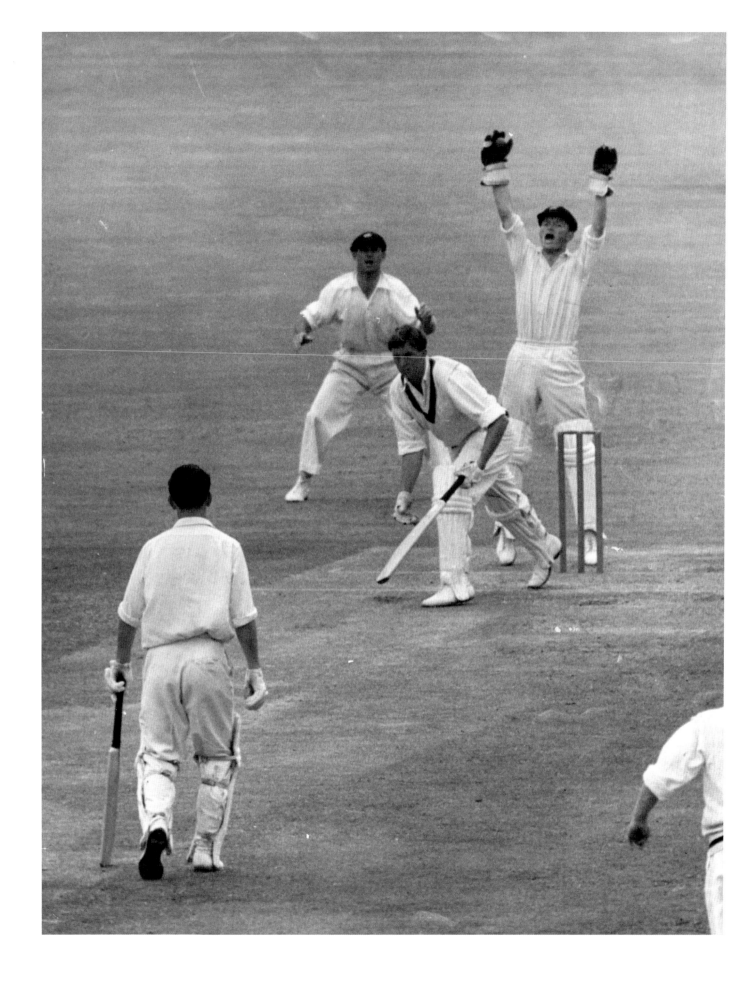

ABOVE The then World's best all-round cricketer, Keith Miller bows after cutting English fast bowler Brain Statham down the gully past Colin Cowdrey at the Sydney Cricket Ground in the Second Test in the 1954/55 series. Match Scores: England 154 and 296 (P.B.H.May 104, M.C.Cowdrey 54); Australia 228 (R.G.Archer 49, J.W.Burke 44, F.H.Tyson 4 for 45, T.E.Bailey 4 for 59) and 184 (R.N.Harvey 92, F.H.Tyson 6 for 85). England won by 38 runs.

LEFT The big-hitting Peter Burge in 1955. Few Australians, or anybody for that matter, have hit the ball harder. A fierce driver, puller and hooker, Burge scored 14640 runs at an average of 47.53 in his first-class career and represented Australia in 42 Test, scoring 2290 runs at 38.16.

ABOVE Fans waiting for the gates to open to get the best seats available outside the Sydney Cricket Ground in 1955.

ABOVE Ian Johnson with Frank Worrell at his right, D.S.Atkinson at his left and the two umpires to Worrell's right looking at the wicket during the 1955 tour to the West Indies.

LEFT Former West Indian player Allan Rae (Jamaica) and Ian Johnson (Australia), the two captains toss in a tour match in July, 1955. Rae had played Test cricket from 1948 to 1953, and was a left-handed top order batsman.

OPPOSITE While they waited for a decision whether play could take place in the Fifth Test at the Sydney Cricket Ground in February, 1955, Australian captain Ian Johnson (right) and English vice-captain Peter May signed autograph books. A rain-drenched Sydney saw no start to play until 2pm on day four. Match Scores: England 371 for 7 dec (T.W.Graveney 111, D.C.S.Compton 84, P.B.H.May 79, T.E.Bailey 72); Australia 221 (C.C.McDonald 72, J.H.Wardle 5 for 79) and 118 for 6. Match drawn.

With the first four Tests all drawn it came down to the Oval Test to see if a result could be managed.

Captains Ian Johnson (Australia) and Len Hutton (England) were thwarted by the Sydney wet in the Fifth Test of 1955. Play was due to start on the 25th February, but the conditions held up the start until well into day four. The series was not a good one for Australia, losing to England 3-1, with the pace duo of Tyson and Statham too good for Australia's batsmen.

Jim Laker, who formed one half of the deadly spin duo, of laker and Lock, that wrested the Ashes away from Australia after 19 years with a Fifth Test win in 1953. With the first four Tests all drawn it came down to the Oval Test to see if a result could be managed. Match Scores: Australia 275 (R.R.Lindwall 62, A.L.Hassett 53, F.S.Trueman 4 for 86) and 162 (R.G.Archer 49, G.A.R.Lock 5 for 45, J.C.Laker 4 for 75); England 306 (L.Hutton 82, T.E.Bailey 64, R.R.Lindwall 4 for 70) and 132 for 2 (W.J.Edrich 55). England won by 8 wickets.

Jim Laker had re-written the record book in this match amid much debate about the preparation of the pitch.

OPPOSITE TOP England's Tony Lock bowling to Australia's Colin McDonald in the First Test at Trent Bridge on the 1956 Ashes Tour. In the days before helmets and body armour, McDonald was an unflinching player to pace and able to read spin. He demonstrated both attributes on this difficult tour to England, in which Australia did not reach 300 in innings in any of the five Test matches. In the famous Fourth Test where Australia was almost 'bowled Laker', (Laker took 19-90) McDonald was the only batsman to show any resistance, with a well compiled 89.

OPPOSITE BELOW Day one of the Australian's match against the MCC in May, 1956. At the end of the first day's play Australia were 334 for 3 wickets, with R.N.Harvey 194 n.o. The photo shows: Peter Burge (Australia) bowled by Fred Titmus for 29.

ABOVE Fourth Test in 1956 at Old Trafford, and R.N.Harvey (Australia) throws his bat in the air in disgust as he is caught Cowdrey, bowled Laker, for a duck in the second innings. In a most unhappy match for Harvey and Australia, he was also bowled Laker for a duck in the first innings. Jim Laker, whose match figues were 68 overs, 27 maidens, 90 runs for 19 wickets, had re-written the record book in this match amid much debate about the preparation of the pitch. Match Scores: England 459 (D.S.Sheppard 113, P.E.Richardson 104, M.C.Cowdrey 80, T.G.Evans 47, P.B.H.May 43, I.W.Johnson 4 for 151); Australia 84 (J.C.Laker 9 for 37) and 205 (C.C.McDonald 89, J.C.Laker 10 for 53). England won by an innings and 170 runs.

ABOVE Australia's Peter Burge is out lbw to J.H.Wardle for a duck, during Australia's first innings in the match against Yorkshire at Bradford, May 1956.

OPPOSITE TOP AND BOTTOM Ian Johnson, played 45 Tests for Australia from 1945 to 1957 and was captain on 17 occasions. He took over captaincy when England were a much stronger outfit than in previous years, and he had the unfortunate record of leading Australia to successive Ashes defeats in 1954/55 and 1956. He was an off-spin bowler and capable bat, who completed the double of 100 Test wickets and 1000 Test runs.

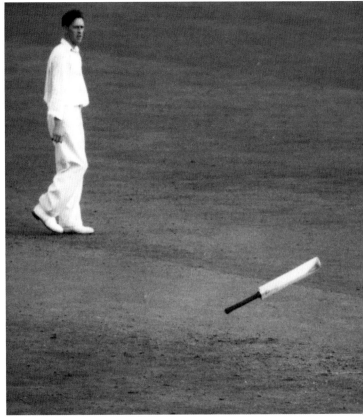

OPPOSITE TOP
Despite these troubled times for Johnson both on and off the field, he remained always ready to please his fans. On the field, in England, he had to contend with dubiously prepared pitches for the English spinners Laker and Lock. While off the field he had to contend with an undercurrent of unrest amongst his players, that Keith Miller was more deserving of the captaincy.

OPPOSITE BOTTOM LEFT
Unusual partnership by two Australian Test cricket personalities … Ian Johnson (right), captain of the present touring team (when photo was taken), and Lindsay Hassett, his predecessor in the Australian captaincy, sing 'The Kangaroo Hop' duet at the Savoy Hotel, London, at 1.30am. They were at the ball, named 'The Kangaroo Hop', held by Australia's touring cricketers in aid of the Cheshire Homes for incurably sick people. Mr. Hassett was Chairman of the ball and Mr. Johnson one of the Vice-Presidents. The Homes were founded by Group-Captain Leonard Cheshire, VC, July, 1956.

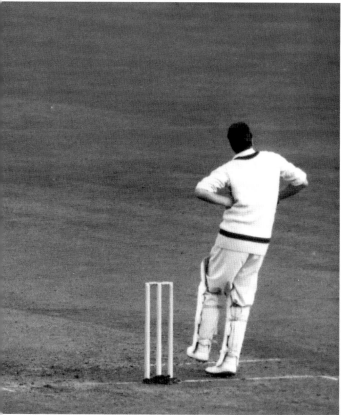

LEFT
Keith Miller winces after being struck on the body from a ball by Brian Statham (also seen). An incident during the second day of the fifth and final Test at the Oval in 1956. Match Scores: England 247 (D.C.S.Compton 94, P.B.H.May 83, R.G.Archer 5 for 53, K.R.Miller 4 for 91) and 182 doe 3 dec (D.S.Sheppard 62); Australia 202 (K.R.Miller 61, J.C.Laker 4 for 80) and 27 for 5. Match drawn.

ABOVE
Jubilant Johnson is delighted as Barrington is caught by Miller off Johnson's bowling during the second day of the final Test at the Oval, 1956. Barrington had batted tediously for over an hour for just four runs.

TOP Australia's captain, Ian
Johnson, shakes hands with his
host, the Duke of Norfolk (right)
before the match between the
Australians and the Duke of
Norfolk's X1 at Arundel castle,
Surrey, April, 1956.

BOTTOM Up goes the coin as rival
captains, the Reverend David
Sheppard, of the Duke of Norfolk's
X1 (left) and Ian Johnson, of the
Australians.

TOP Third Test Match at Headingley. Keith Miller, the Australian batsman, and Evans, the England wicketkeeper, in a tangle, as Miller tries to regain his crease and Evans tries to get the ball.

BOTTOM Australian Test cricketers Ian Johnson (left), captain, and Keith Miller, vice-captain, proudly display their M.B.E.'s after they had attended an investiture ceremony at Buckingham Palace, July, 1956.

ABOVE MCC v Australia at Lords, May, 1956. Congratulations from the MCC captain, R.T.Simpson, and vanquished MCC bowler, Moss, Neil Harvey and J. Rutherford. The Australian's had combined to put on 218 for the second wicket.

LEFT Former Australian Test star, Bill Ponsford walks out to bat at St.Kilda cricket ground, Melbourne. Ponsford, then 56 years-of-age, captained a team of former State and Test cricketers which defeated a similar team led by Lindsay Hassett. The game raised more than 100 pounds for the V.C.A. players provident fund, February, 1957.

OPPOSITE TOP Australian cricketers in the past have seldom received the Benefit matches awarded their English counterparts. But in January, 1957, Stan McCabe (right) and Bill O'Reilly (left), leave the SCG with NSW Cricket Association President Syd Smith during the Benefit match for this great Test duo.

OPPOSITE BOTTOM: You can't have a Testimonial without some fun, and here Bill O'Reilly still thinks he's a better bowler than Stan McCabe was a batsman. Harvey and Lindwall are interested players in the slips.

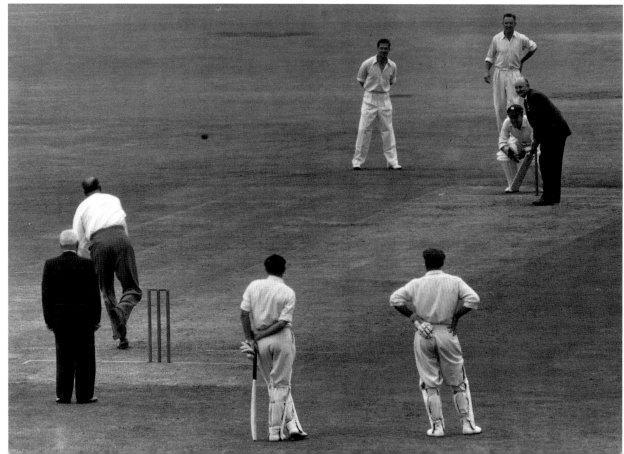

ABOVE Former Test cricket stars Bill O'Reilly, Stan McCabe and Frank Cush (President of the Australian Cricket Board) watch the proceedings at the Testimonial Match at the SCG in 1957.

OPPOSITE Stan McCabe in his famous sports store in the Sydney CBD. Like many cricketers of the day, he turned his sporting notoriety into a popular sporting goods store, that was frequented by many an admiring youngster.

... he turned his sporting notoriety into a popular sporting goods store

OPPOSITE West Indies leading spin bowler Sonny Ramadhin in practice at the SCG No.2 nets in preparation for the Second Test of the 1951 tour. His only good return in the Tests that summer was in the First Test when he captured 5 for 90 in the second innings. For the remainder of the series he struggled to make an impression.

ABOVE It's January, 1957 at a suburban ground in Sydney and 47 year-old Stan McCabe moves out with all his old-time grace to cover drive one of the 13 boundaries, and one six, in the 68 runs he scored in this well-supported charity match. Behind the stumps is 62 year-old former Test player of the Bodyline series, Hammy Love.

RIGHT M.A.Noble, former leading Australian player, captain, administrator and dentist was engaged by the ABC in the 1950s to supply expert opinion to their cricket coverage on radio.

OPPOSITE Australian cricket captain, Ian Craig and former Test cricketer Bert Oldfield with schoolboys from Knox College, giving the college's First Eleven a few pointers after watching them in action, in February, 1957.

ABOVE Australia's captain, Richie Benaud pulls Laker to the mid-on boundary in the Third Test at the Sydney Cricket Ground in the 1958/59 series. Match Scores: England 219 (P.B.H.May 42, R.Sweetman 41, R.Benaud 5 for 83) and 287 for 7 dec (M.C.Cowdrey 100, P.B.H.May 92, R.Benaud 4 for 94); Australia 357 (N.C.O'Neill 77, A.K.Davidson 71, K.D.Mackay 57, L.E.Favell 54, C.C.McDonald 40, J.C.Laker 5 for 107, G.A.R.Lock 4 for 130) and 54 for 2. Match drawn.

ABOVE 'Fiery Freddie' Trueman fails in his appeal for lbw against little known South Australia batsman, Col Pinch in a tour game in the summer of 1958/59. Trueman, one of England's great bowlers and great characters had a difficult tour against a very strong Australian team. His best return in the Test series was 4 for 90 in the first innings of the Fourth Test at Adelaide and 4 for 92 in the first innings of the Fifth Test at Melbourne.

RIGHT Victorian Colin Crompton about to be caught by New South Wales Richie Benaud in slips off Jim Burke for 4 at the SCG in 1959. Burke, who was better known as a batsman, with three Test centuries in 24 Tests at an average of 34.59, was also a handy right arm off-break bowler for his state side. In 130 first-class games from 1948/49 to 1958/59 he captured over 100 wickets at the healthy average of 29.11.

ABOVE One of Lindwall's greatest moments. He is shown taking the wicket of England's Trevor Bailey in the Fifth Test in the second innings at Melbourne in the summer of 1958/59 to break Clarrie Grimmett's record for most wickets by an Australian in Tests.

ABOVE One-time schoolmates in the impoverished Sydney
suburb of Waterloo, former Governor-General Sir William
McKell and Test great Arthur Mailey relax on the world-
famous hill at the Sydney Cricket Ground in the 1950s.

ABOVE The Australian team claps fast bowler Ian Meckiff from the field after he had routed England in the Second Test of 1958–59 at the Melbourne Cricket Ground. Alan Davidson, cap in hand, leads the applause. Match Scores: England 259 (P.B.H.May 113, T.E.Bailey 48, M.C.Cowdrey 44, A.K.Davidson 6 for 64) and 87 (I.Meckiff 6 for 38); Australia 308 (R.N.Harvey 167, C.C.McDonald 47, J.B.Statham 7 for 57) and 42 for 2. Australia won by 8 wickets.

Fast bowler Ian Meckiff routed England in the Second Test of 1958–59

ABOVE The popular Norman O'Neill shows the intense concentration he applies to his stroke making. His quick mastery of slower English wickets was a testimony to his concentration and ability to overcome difficult playing conditions. He played for Australia in 42 Tests, scoring 2,779 runs at an average of 45.55, with a high score of 181. He also chipped in with 17 wickets at 39.23.

OPPOSITE TOP Richie Benaud relaxing by bowling barefooted to his son in the backyard of his then home at Beecroft, Sydney.

OPPOSITE BOTTOM Colin McDonald plays his favourite backcut, a shot which brought him hundreds of runs in all classes of cricket. He played 47 Tests from 1952 to 1961, scoring 3107 runs at an average of 39.32, with a topscore of 170. His first-class record of 11375 runs at an average of 40.48 was achieved over 192 games from 1947–48 to 1962–63.

Neil Harvey, a member of the touring team for the upcoming to South Africa in 1957/58, 'fills-in' for the Australian team manager, Mr. J. Janike, who withdrew from the tour because of illness. Harvey is shown issuing flight folders and gear to team-members Ian

1960 – 1969

6

1960

THE 1960S WAS A DECADE OF ENORMOUS SOCIAL CHANGE — influenced as they were the explosion in youth 'pop' culture, the development of permissive sexual attitudes and Australia's involvement in the Vietnam War. As the nation celebrated New Years Day in 1960, Australia was still something of a conservative stronghold with Liberal Prime Minister Bob Menzies entering his third decade in power (1949–1966). As the decade opened Australian cricket was in the middle of its tour of India, having already defeated Pakistan in a three-Test series. On January 1, 1960 Ritchie Benaud led Australia in the third Test in Bombay, with the visitors already having won the first Test in Delhi by an innings and 27 runs a month before. Although the match ended in a draw, after centuries to N.J.Contractor (106) and Australians Neil Harvey (102) and Norm O'Neill (163), Australia won the fourth Test in Madras and ultimately recorded a 2–1 result in the five-Test series.

The match ended in a tie — and jubilation amongst the West Indian players, disappointment in the Australian camp

But 1960 will forever be remembered for the historic tied Test match — the first tie in international Test history — between Australia and the West Indies in the first Test in Brisbane. When the match started in the second week of December, a brilliant 132 from West Indian master Gary Sobers on the opening day of play set the scene for a memorable Test. Australia responded to the West Indies' first innings total of 453 with an impressive 505. When Benaud's men bowled the visitors out for 284 — requiring a score of 232 to win on the last day of play — Australia started its chase in earnest. At tea Australia was struggling at 6/92, but then went after the impossible. Benaud and Davidson put on 50 before the drinks break and another 84 afterwards before the partnership was broken at 7/226 when Davidson was run out with just two overs to go. Benaud (52) and Grout (2) fell in the final over of the match after pushing the score to 9/232. With Ian Meckiff and Lindsay Kline at the crease, West Indian fieldsman Joe Solomons threw down the stumps at the danger end as Meckiff scurried through for what would have been the winning run. The match ended in a tie — and jubilation amongst the West Indian players, disappointment in the Australian camp and momentary confusion amongst the Brisbane crowd and huge TV and radio audience. It did not immediately sink in that the Test had in fact ended in a tie.

Australia ultimately won the fifth Test and the series, 2–1 — with one test drawn and of course, one tied — but such was the impact that Frank Worrell's West Indian team had on the Australian public that the Australian Board of Control donated a perpetual trophy for future Test matches between the two nations. Named the 'Frank Worrell Trophy', the prize honoured an international sporting team that arrived in Australia unheralded but left these shores as heroes. Such was the charm, sportsmanship and skill of the West Indian team — captained by the gentlemanly Frank Worrell — that many see the 1960-61 West Indian tour as playing an important role in the breaking down of deep-seated racism in this country. The Australian and West Indian teams were even given a ticker-tape parade in Melbourne after the series was completed in February 1961. As far as Australian fans were concerned, the West Indian players were The Beatles of international cricket.

In June 1961 Ritchie Benaud led Australia to England to defend the Ashes. Victorian batsmen Bill Lawry, playing in only his second Test, scored 130 in Australia's second Test victory at Lords. Although Peter May's England team bounced back to win the third Test at Headingly (highlighted by Freddie Trueman's 5/16 in a six-over spell) another ton by Lawry (102) set up a 54 run win at Old Trafford in the fourth Test and saw the Ashes safely retained. Wally Grout set a new record for Australian wicket keepers when he captured his 21st dismissal in the series which beat the previous record set by Don Tallon in 1946–47.

Imported players such as Caribbean fast bowler Wes Hall (playing for Queensland), and premier batsmen Gary Sobers (South Australia) and Rohan Hanhai (Western Australia) boosted Australia's domestic Sheffield Shield season in 1961–62 before England arrived the following summer in search of Ashes success. After leading Australia to series wins against India, Pakistan, the West Indies and a successful Ashes defence in England, Ritchie Benaud led Australia to a 1–all series draw in the 1962–63 Ashes contest. Captained by Ted Dexter, England won the second Test in Melbourne by seven wickets but Australia responded with an 8 wicket victory in Sydney in the New Year. With three drawn Test matches in the five-Test series, the Ashes result may have been somewhat different had England held on to its catches but centuries by Harvey (154) and O'Neill (100) in Adelaide and Peter Burge (103) in Sydney proved Australia's superiority at home.

the Ashes result may have been somewhat different had England held on to its catches

The South African tour of Australia in the summer of 1963-64 started sensationally in Brisbane when Australian bowler Ian Meckiff — recalled to the Australian team by selectors for the first time since the series against the West Indies three years before — was no-balled four times in his first over by square leg umpire Col Eager. Meckiff had been no-balled during the 1958–59 Ashes series, and in Shield cricket the previous year, but this decision rocked the Australian team and Meckiff did not bowl again in the innings. Although supported by the parochial Brisbane crowd, who chaired the forlorn bowler from the field at the end of the incident-packed second day's play, Meckiff did not bowl again in the match and his international career was over. The series was poised 1–all as Australia approached the fifth Test in Sydney. Billed as Ritchie Benaud's swansong, the match finished in a draw and kept the Australian captain's unbeaten Test-series record against all cricketing nations intact.

Following Benaud's retirement, Bobby Simpson led Australia in its defence of the Ashes in England in 1964. With the first two Tests finishing in tame draws because of the inclement

1969

1960

English weather, Australia won the third Test at Headingly by 7 wickets on the back of Peter Burge's 160. Simpson's mighty 311 at Old Trafford (overshadowing fellow opener Bill Lawry's 106) in Australia's 8/656 declared was matched by England's 611 (Barrington, 256 and Dexter, 174) and led to a predictable draw and the retainment of the Ashes. The fifth Test at the Oval also finished in a soggy draw but two milestones were passed; England opener Geoff Boycott scored his first century on home soil and Fred Trueman became the first bowler to pass 300 Test wickets. The tour finished with a major shock when Australia was defeated by Holland in a one-day match at The Hague. Australia was all out for 197 (Jack Potter received a fractured skull in the match) which was bettered by Holland's 7/201.

Australia drew a three-Test series against India in October 1964 before playing a one-off Test against Pakistan in Karachi. When the match also finished in a draw, Pakistan agreed to the suggestion by the Victorian Cricket Association that a proposed tour game against Victoria the following December be changed to a Test match. South Australian batsman Ian Chappell, the grandson of former test captain Vic Richardson, made his debut alongside bowler David Sincock in the Melbourne Test on 4 December. The Test against Pakistan, the first played between the two nations in Australia, finished in a dour draw watched by a combined crowd of just 33,000 people.

> *The tour finished with a major shock when Australia was defeated by Holland in a one-day match at The Hague.*

The West Indies won the inaugural Frank Worrell Trophy when Australia toured there in 1965. The home-side won the first and third Tests and with the second Test drawn Australia desperately needed a result in the fourth Test of the series. Australia got off to a magnificent start with double centuries to openers Bill Lawry and captain Bob Simpson (posting an opening stand of 382) but not even a daring declaration, which left the West Indies with 253 to win on the last day of play, could forced a result. Australia finished the tour with a convincing 10-wicket victory in the fifth-Test at Port-of-Spain but Simpson presented the Frank Worrell Trophy to West Indian captain Gary Sobers despite Australia's belated victory in the series.

19-year-old Australian batsmen Doug Walters and England bowler Bob Barber were the sensations of the 1965-66 Ashes series in Australia but with two drawn Tests to open the series, England took an early advantage with an innings and 93 run victory in the Third Test in Sydney. It was Lawry (119) and Simpson (225) who saved the Ashes, with a 244 opening run partnership in the fourth Test at Adelaide. Australia won the match by an innings and 9 runs before a masterful 307 by Australian batsman Bob Cowper (surpassing Don Bradman's 299 not out as the highest total ever registered on Australian soil) ground the fifth Test in Melbourne to a draw.

South Africa proved its superiority over Australia in the southern hemisphere summer of 1966-67 with a 3–1 series win at home. Described as 'the worst ever' Australian team to tour oversees by former captain turned broadcaster Ritchie Benaud, the fact that the visitors lost three of the five Tests played tended to support Benaud's opinion. Australia was on the back foot after a shock loss in the first Test in Johannesburg but after a 6 wicket win in the second Test (centuries by Simpson and Keith Stackpole were answered by a faultless 209 from Graeme Pollock), on-field tension with local umpires and criticism of Bob Simpson's leadership seemed to rattle the Australian captain. Simpson stood his ground when given out in the fourth Test but showed his graciousness after Australia's loss in the fifth Test when he presented South African captain Peter Van der Merwe with his baggy green cap as a memento of the series.

Australia welcomed a new captain in the second half of the domestic Test series against India in 1967–68 with Bill Lawry taking over after the retirement of Bill Simpson. After scoring another century alongside Lawry in Australia's second Test victory in Melbourne, 32-year-old Simpson stood down as Test captain. Although he declared his availability for the remainder of the series, Simpson was not chosen in either Test. Selectors also showed that they were looking towards the Ashes series in England in 1968 when they rested in-form West Australian bowler 'Garth' McKenzie from the last two Tests in order to trial other bowlers. Bill Lawry's teams completed the 4–0, clean sweep of India before leading Australia to England the following June.

Lawry answered criticism of his dour style with a fighting 135 in Australia's response to England's 494

After a 159 run victory in the first Test at Old Trafford, three Ashes Tests were drawn. In the second Test of the series Australia marked the 200th Test between the two nations with a farcical 9 declared for 78 in response to England's first innings total of 351 in a weather-marred match at Lords. Lawry was ruled out of the deciding fourth Test with a broken figure (England captain Colin Cowdrey was also ruled out of the match) but wicketkeeper Barry Jarman ably deputised for his captain. England won the fifth Test by 226 runs but Lawry answered criticism of his dour style with a fighting 135 in Australia's response to England's 494 — and also, by retaining the Ashes.

Australia confirmed its mantle as the No. 1 cricket-playing nation in the world with a hard-fought, 3–1 Test series win over the West Indies in 1968–69. Australia claimed a 2–1 lead in the series with a 10 wicket victory in the third Test in Sydney. Following another drawn result, in Adelaide, Australia went into the fifth match of the series needing a win or a draw to claim the Frank Worrell Trophy. NSW batsmen Doug Walters chose this moment to lay claim as the most exciting young batsman of his generation when he scored 242 in the first innings and 103 in the second (thus becoming the first cricketer to score a double century and a century in a Test match) before an appreciative Sydney crowd.

A 3–1 Test series victory against India (the last series win by an Australian team in India for 35 years) closed a remarkable decade in Australian cricket. Australia had maintained its standing as one of the pre-eminent cricketing nations in the word during a decade of incredible social and cultural change but in the 1970s the game would prove not so immune to the political and economic forces that affected the rest of the world.

1969

ABOVE Bill Lawry is congratulated by work-mates in his days as a plumber. A left-handed opening batsman, he debuted for Australia on the 1961 Ashes tour to England in 1961, scoring a century in each of the Tests Australia won, an indominatble 130 on an exacting ridge at Lord's and 102 in Fourth Test at Old Trafford. As courageous a batsman as he was, by the time he was appointed captain of Australia, against India in 1967/68, he had become the most rigidly self-denying batsman of his era, who was as hard to watch as he was to dismiss.

LEFT Sonny Ramadhin jokes with his West Indies team-mates in Brisbane during the early part of the 1960/61 tour to Australia. Rohan Kanhai (third from right) and Garfield Sobers (sitting on railing) seem to be instigating the players amusing response.

ABOVE Wally Grout makes a spectacular dive to catch West Indian Lance Gibbs during the Third Test at Sydney in the summer of 1960/61, the Windies only Test win of the series. Match Scores: West Indies 339 (G.S.Sobers 168, A.K.Davidson 5 for 80, R.Benaud 4 for 86) and 326 (F.C.M.Alexander 108, F.M.M.Worrell 82, C.W.Smith 55, R.Benaud 4 for 113); Australia 202 (N.C.O'Neill 71, A.L.Valentine 4 for 67) and 241 (R.N.Harvey 85, N.C.O'Neill 70, L.R.Gibbs 5 for 66, A.L.Valentine 4 for 86). West Indies won by 222 runs.

ABOVE The controversial dismissal of West Indian Joe Solomon during the West Indies v. Australia Test series of 1960/61 in the Second Test at Melbourne. Australian wicketkeeper Wally Grout is pointing to Solomon's cap, which dislodged a bail during the stroke. The West Indians agreed that the decision that Solomon was out was correct, but that did not stop a nationwide debate, sparked by the press of the day. Match Scores: Australia 348 (K.D.Mackay 74, J.W.Martin 55, L.E.Favell 51, W.W.Hall 4 for 51) and 70 for 3; West Indies 181 (R.Kanhai 84, S.M.Nurse 70, A.K.Davidson 6 for 53) and 233 (C.C.Hunte 110, F.C.M.Alexander 72). Australia won by 7 wickets.

RIGHT A great shot of the Sydney Cricket Ground, during the Third Test, in January, 1961. With the grandstands packed, as is usually the case in Sydney, and with the hill in the background this ground has been long regarded as the perfect size for Test cricket.

RIGHT Alan Davidson, Australia's great fast bowler from 1953 to 1963. A left-arm paceman with a model approach, he shows his characteristic hop after bowling, left knee bent, weight on right toe. He played 44 Tests for Australia, capturing 186 wickets at an average of 20.53. He was also a very handy left-handed batsman, scoring 1328 runs at an average of 24.59, with 5 fifties, with his high score of 80 achieved in the second innings of the famous Tied Test at Brisbane in December, 1961.

The New South Wales Cricket Association reception given to the West Indies cricketers in November, 1960. The photo shows fast bowlers Gordon Rorke from Australia on the left and the West Indies Wesley Hall on the right.

West Indian thunderbolt Wes Hall slams another down the pitch. The day before he had claimed five of the Australian wickets to fall in the famous Tied Test in Brisbane in the 1960/61 series. Match Scores: West Indies 453 (G.S.Sobers 132, F.M.M.Worrell 65, J.S.Solomon 65, F.C.M.Alexander 60, W.W.Hall 50; A.K.Davidson 5 for 153) and 284 (F.M.M.Worrell 65, R.Kanhai 54, A.K.Davidson 6 for 87): Australia 505 (N.C.O'Neill 181, R.B.Simpson 92, C.C.McDonald 57, W.W.Hall 4 for 140) and 232 (A.K.Davidson 80, R.Benaud 62, W.W.Hall 5 for 63). Match Tied.

LEFT Australian Test spinner Lindsay Kline splendidly caught in the middle of the 'Kangaroo hop' which was part of his left-arm delivery. He might have represented Australia in just 13 Tests, but it was an eventful Test career. He took a hat-trick in his second Test, in Cape Town in 1957/58, was the batsman that faced the last ball of the Tied Test against the West Indies at Brisbane in 1960/61 and also batted for 100 minutes as Australia held on for a draw at Adelaide in the same series.

BELOW West Indian captain Frank Worrell bowling to Australian Lindsay Kline at Adelaide, in the Fourth Test in the summer of 1960/61. With all ten fieldsmen around the bat, Kline defied the West Indians to save a match that seemed lost. Match Scores: West Indies 393 (R.Kanhai 117, F.M.M.Worrell 71, F.C.M.Alexander 63, R.Benaud 5 for 96) and 432 for 6 dec (R.Kanhai 115, F.C.M.Alexander 87, C.C.Hunte 79, F.M.M.Worrell 53); Australia 366 (R.B.Simpson 85, R.Benaud 77, C.C.McDonald 71, L.R.Gibbs 5 for 97) and 273 for 9 (N.C.O'Neill 65, K.D.Mackay 62). Match Drawn.

ABOVE Spectators farewell the West Indies players at the Melbourne Cricket Ground after the exciting Fifth Test in 1961. Match Scores: West Indies 292 (G.S.Sobers 64, F.M.Misson 4 for 58) and 321 (F.C.M.Alexander 73, C.C.Hunte 52, A.K.Davidson 5 for 84); Australia 356 (C.C.McDonald 91, R.B.Simpson 75, P.J.Burge 68, G.S.Sobers 5 for 120, L.R.Gibbs 4 for 74) and 258 for 8 (R.B.Simpson 92, P.J.Burge 53). Australia won by 2 wickets.

BELOW The members of the 1961 Australian cricket team leaving Sydney by air for Melbourne on their way for a three-day match in Launceston before going on to England. Walking to the plane at Kingsford Smith Airport are (left to right): Bobby Simpson, Brian Booth, Neil Harvey, Frank Misson, captain Richie Benaud, and team manager Mr S.G.Webb.

ABOVE West Indian speedster Wesley Hall bowls to Australian Colin McDonald, during the Third Test of the 1960/61 series at Sydney, in a perfect example of an umbrella field. Count the fieldsmen behind the wicket and note the open spaces in front of the batsman.

BELOW The West Indians jubilantly appeal for an lbw decision against Australian opener Colin McDonald. Neil Harvey is the other batsman, in a thrilling moment from the 1960-61 Test series in Australia, a series still regarded as the best ever. McDonald scored 337 runs in that series, at an average of 33.7, with a high score of 91 in the Fifth Test at Melbourne.

OPPOSITE RIGHT Alf Valentine in action in the nets at the Sydney Cricket Ground No 2. in February, 1961. While not the force he was on his previous tour to Australia (in 1951/52), he still provided solid support to the West Indian trumps of Hall, Gibbs and Sobers.

ABOVE Eric Freeman's powerful hit soars through the air on its way through the Victor Richardson Memorial Gates and into the street outside in the Fourth Test of the 1968/69 series. The six pairs of eyes, riveted in awe, belong to Freeman, wicketkeeper Jackie Hendriks, Garfield Sobers (right background), bowler Lance Gibbs, umpire Col Egar and Freeman's batting Doug Walters. Match Scores: West Indies 276 (G.S.Sobers 110, B.F.Butcher 52, E.W.Freeman 4 for 52) and 616 (B.F.Butcher 118, M.C.Carew 90, R.Kanhai 80, D.A.J.Holford 80, G.S.Sobers 52, A.N.Connolly 5 for 122); Australia 533 (K.D.Walters 110, I.M.Chappell 76, W.M.Lawry 62, K.R.Stackpole 62, G.D.McKenzie 59, A.P.Sheahan 51, L.R.Gibbs 4 for 145) and 339 for 9 (I.M.Chappell 96, W.M.Lawry 89, K.R.Stackpole 50, K.D.Walters 50) Match drawn.

RIGHT West Indies captain Frank Worrell playing soccer with a tennis ball at the Gabba ground, Brisbane, on 8th December, 1960. The following day the First Test would start, and the Australian public would be captivated by the events that unfolded.

BELOW Seymour Nurse, the Barbados batsman, steps forward for an on-drive off Sonny Ramadhin at practice at the Brisbane Cricket Ground. Nurse, a middle order batsman, who debuted against England in the 1959/60 series, was a powerfully-built batsman and excellent fieldsman. While his Test aggregrate of 2523 at 47.6, was impressive enough, in his last Test match (against New Zealand in 1968/69) he thumped a magnificent 258.

Seymour Nurse from Barbados was a powerfully-built batsman and excellent fieldsman.

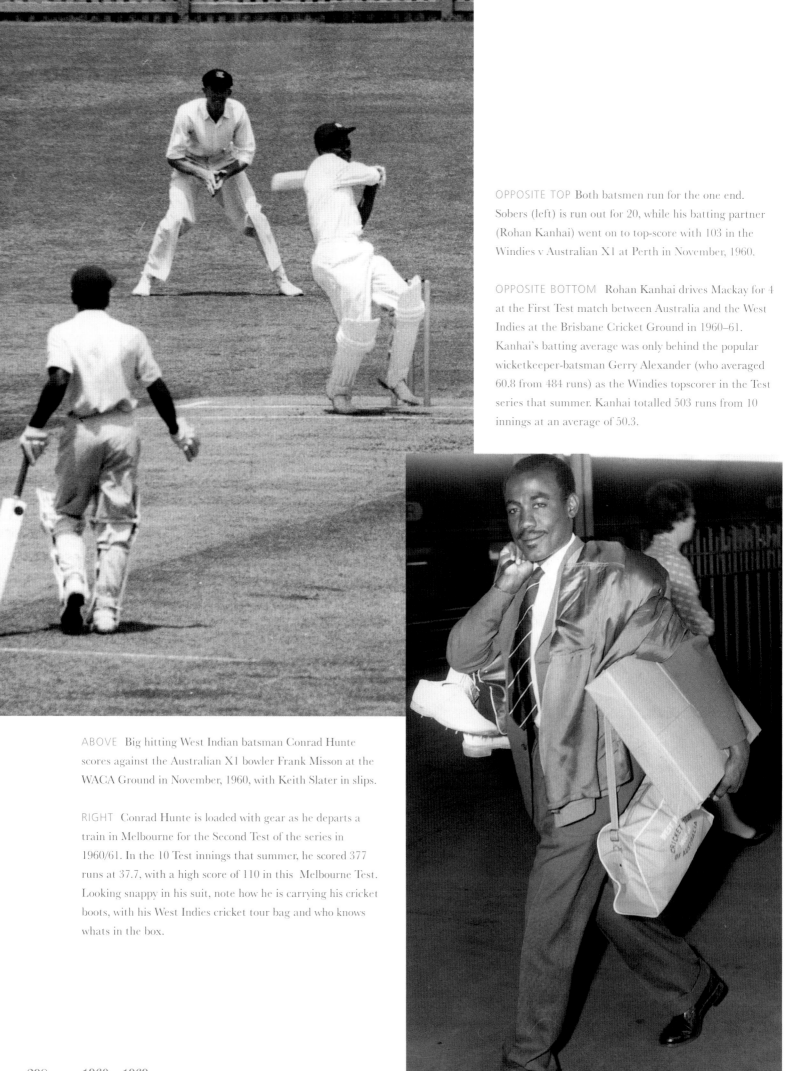

OPPOSITE TOP Both batsmen run for the one end. Sobers (left) is run out for 20, while his batting partner (Rohan Kanhai) went on to top-score with 103 in the Windies v Australian X1 at Perth in November, 1960.

OPPOSITE BOTTOM Rohan Kanhai drives Mackay for 4 at the First Test match between Australia and the West Indies at the Brisbane Cricket Ground in 1960–61. Kanhai's batting average was only behind the popular wicketkeeper-batsman Gerry Alexander (who averaged 60.8 from 484 runs) as the Windies topscorer in the Test series that summer. Kanhai totalled 503 runs from 10 innings at an average of 50.3.

ABOVE Big hitting West Indian batsman Conrad Hunte scores against the Australian X1 bowler Frank Misson at the WACA Ground in November, 1960, with Keith Slater in slips.

RIGHT Conrad Hunte is loaded with gear as he departs a train in Melbourne for the Second Test of the series in 1960/61. In the 10 Test innings that summer, he scored 377 runs at 37.7, with a high score of 110 in this Melbourne Test. Looking snappy in his suit, note how he is carrying his cricket boots, with his West Indies cricket tour bag and who knows whats in the box.

OPPOSITE TOP West Indies captain, Frank Worrell with Australia's captain Richie Benaud in deep conversation at the reception for the West Indies team in November, 1960. They could be saying, 'lets have a series that everyone will remember'.

OPPOSITE BOTTOM Team-mates surround Lance Gibbs to congratulate him after dismissing Frank Misson to complete his history-making hat-trick the Fourth Test at Adelaide in 1960/61. He had been left out of the first two Tests, and had taken three wickets in four balls in Sydney. A great spinner of the ball, he took 309 Test wickets in 79 Tests at an average of 29.09. He was always heavily relied on, bowling at astonishing 27,115 deliveries in Tests, conceding only a miserly 1.99 runs per over.

RIGHT TOP Spectators witnessed a spectacular attempt by Australia's Neil Harvey to regain his ground in a match against Worcester on the 1961 tour. Harvey had been metres outside, but somehow made his ground, despite a smart return to Worcester keeper, Booth.

RIGHT BOTTOM England players breathe a huge sigh of relief as D.A. Allen bowls Peter Burge for 181, the highest score of the tour, in Australia's first innings on the third day of the Fifth Test at the Oval. It was Burge's first Test century against England. Match Scores: England 256 (P.B.H.May 71, K.F.Barrington 53, A.K.Davidson 4 for 83) and 370 (R.Subba Row 137, K.F.Barrington 83, D.A.Allen 42, J.T.Murray 40, K.D.Mackay 5 for 121); Australia 494 (P.J.P.Burge 181, N.C.O'Neill 117, B.C.Booth 71, R.B.Simpson 40, D.A.Allen 4 for 133). Match drawn.

OPPOSITE   Wes Hall (left) and Alf Valentine leave the field after Hall was out for 10, which was the last wicket to fall in their first innings total of 339 in the Third Test at Sydney. Hall, who was a real number 11 batsman, always adopted the theory of 'hit out or get out'.

TOP   Les Favell is caught Worrell bowled Valentine for 16 during the Third Test at Sydney in 1960/61. Favell played 19 Tests for Australia from 1954 to 1961, scoring 757 runs at an average of 27.03, with a top score of 101 (his only Test century).

BOTTOM   Les Favell, one of the faster scoring Australian batsmen of the postwar period, never converted his success at first-class level to the Test arena. His first-class record was: 12379 runs at an average of 36.63, with a top score of 190, scoring 27 centuries and 67 half-centuries.

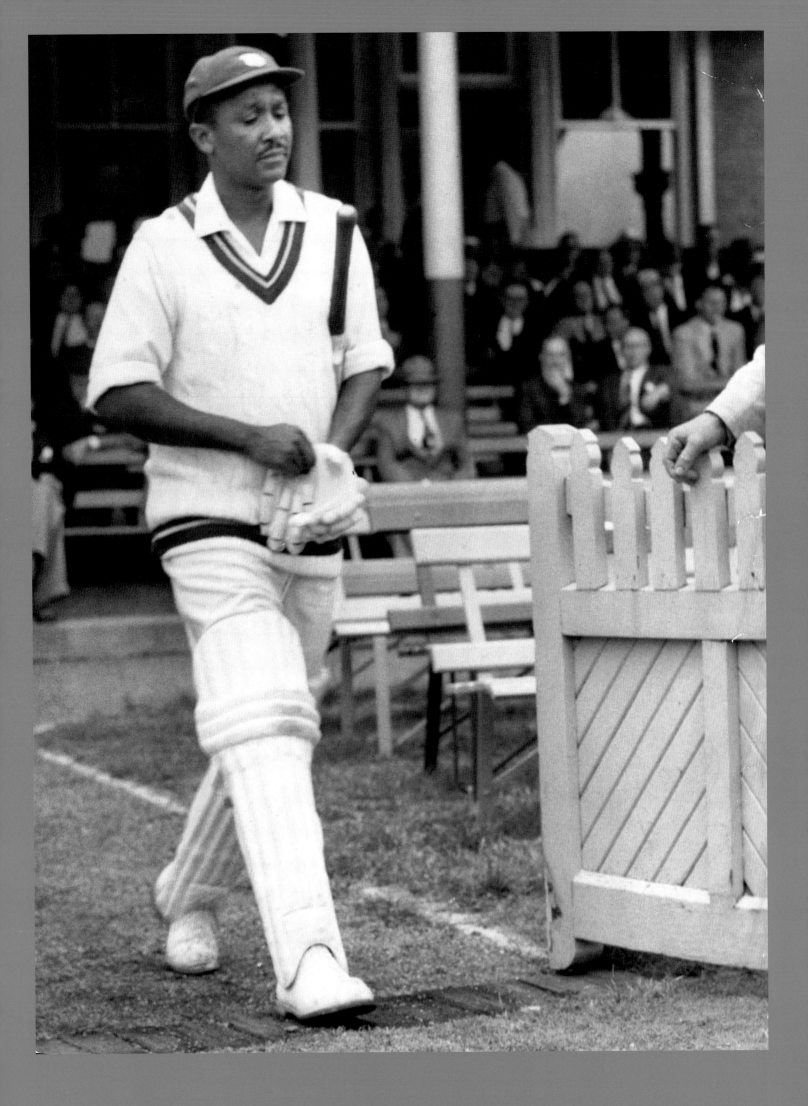

OPPOSITE Frank Worrell goes out to bat in his team's only Test win of the 1960/61 series. His 82 in the second innings helped set Australia a target of 464 to win, with the Windies eventuall dismissing them for 241. Match Scores: West Indies 339 (G.S.Sobers 168, A.K.Davidson 5 for 80, R.Benaud 4 for 86) and 326 (F.C.M.Alexander 108, F.M.M.Worrell 82, C.W.Smith 55, R.Benaud 4 for 113); Australia 202 (N.C.O'Neill 71, A.L.Valentine 4 for 67) and 241 (R.N.Harvey 85, N.C.O'Neill 70, L.R.Gibbs 5 for 66, A.L.Valentine 4 for 86). West Indies won by 222 runs.

ABOVE Graham McKenzie, the young Western Australian and Australian fast-medium bowler who had taken 100 Test wickets by the age of 23. Four years later, at still only 27 he had taken that tally to 200. In an era of benign pitches, his achievement was even more exemplary, but his enthusiasm eventually wained and he retired from the Test scene to play county cricket with Leicestershire in England. In all he played in 60 Tests from 1961 to 1971, capturing 246 wickets at an average of 29.78, with a career best of 8 for 71 against the West Indies at Melbourne in 1968/69.

OPPOSITE Another West Indian tourist from the 1960/61 series, must have liked what he saw here on tour. He returned to play Shield cricket for Queensland, who he played 16 matches for, over the summers of 1961 to 1963. Here tearaway star bowler Wes Hall grins broadly as he plays an unorthodox stroke to an awkward ball from New South Wales spinner Johnny Martin, in the Shield match at the SCG yesterday in January, 1962. With the ball almost trickling onto his stumps, wicketkeeper Doug Ford also enjoys the joke.

LEFT West Indian great, Rohan Kanhai seen here playing for Western Australia against New South Wales in November, 1961. He powerfully cover-drives Johnny Martin during his innings of 81 against New South Wales at the SCG. In all he played in 8 games for Western Australia during the summer of 1961/62, scoring 533 runs at an average of 41.

BELOW Here Johnny Martin is in the action again. This time it's November, 1960 and his New South Wales team-mate Graham Thomas takes a smart catch to dismiss the West Indies opener and top-scorer Joe Solomon for 55 in the second innings, off his bowling. New South Wales defeated the seemingly uninterested tourists by an innings and 119 runs. Match Scores: West Indies 111 (F.M.M.Worrell 51, A.K.Davidson 4 for 26, J.Martin 3 for 22) and 199 (J.Solomon 55, R.Benaud 5 for 31, J.Martin 3 for 95); New South Wales 429 for 6 dec (N.C.O'Neill 156, R.N.Harvey 109, A.K.Davidson 88).

ABOVE Barry Jarman whips off the bails in spectacular style to dismiss Grahame Thomas in a New South Wales versus South Australia Sheffield shield match in the 1960s. Thomas, who had made 148, scrambled desperately to regain his crease but Jarman's swiftness gave him no chance. Thomas, who was part American-Indian, played 100 first-class matches from 1957/58 to 1965/66, scored 5726 runs at an average of 40.32, with a high score of 229 against Victoria at Melbourne in 1965/66. While he took part in three tours with the Australia sides, in 1959/60 to New Zealand, 1964/65 to South Africa and 1965/66 to England, he never managed to cement a position in the very strong sides of the day. His only played 8 Tests for 325 runs at 29.54 per innings.

LEFT An excellent example of Australian catching, with Alan Davidson diving forward at short leg to catch Ian Meckiff during a New South Wales versus Victoria in a Sheffield Shield match during the early 1960s.

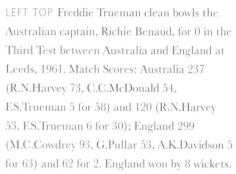

LEFT TOP Freddie Trueman clean bowls the Australian captain, Richie Benaud, for 0 in the Third Test between Australia and England at Leeds, 1961. Match Scores: Australia 237 (R.N.Harvey 73, C.C.McDonald 54, F.S.Trueman 5 for 58) and 120 (R.N.Harvey 53, F.S.Trueman 6 for 30); England 299 (M.C.Cowdrey 93, G.Pullar 53, A.K.Davidson 5 for 63) and 62 for 2. England won by 8 wickets.

LEFT BOTTOM Richie Benaud gets his revenge, catching Freddie Trueman Bob Simpson's bowling, for 8, in England's disastrous second innings on the last day of the Fourth Test at Old Trafford. England collapsed from 150 for 2, to 201 all out, giving Australia victory with just 20 minutes to spare. Match Scores: Australia 190 (W.M.Lawry 74, B.C.Booth 46, J.B.Statham 5 for 53); and 432 (W.M.Lawry 102, A.K.Davidson 77, N.C.O'Neill 67, R.B.Simpson 51, D.A.Allen 4 for 58); England 367 (P.B.H.May 95, K.F.Barrington 78, G.Pullar 63, D.A.Allen 42, R.B.Simpson 4 for 23) and 201 (E.R.Dexter 76, R.Subba Row 49, R.Benaud 6 for 70). Australia won by 54 runs.

ABOVE West Indian master batsman Rohan Kanhai pulls a ball to leg during practice, in 1961, in the true style of the West Indian's cavalier batting approach. Australia was lucky to witness some of their greats at the pinnacle of their carrers when they performed in this country.

BELOW Mr A.G.'Johnnie' Moyes, cricket commentator for the ABC and author casting an expert eye over his beloved SCG during play in the Third Test of the 1962/63 Ashes series. Moyes, unfortunately passed away a short time later.

OPPOSITE Possibly the greatest all-rounder of all-time, West Indies Sir Garfield Sobers. Picture shows him practising in the nets for South Australia's match prior to the clash against New South Wales in January, 1962. Sobers played three seasons for South Australia, during which he achieved twice, an amazing double of 1,000 runs and 50 wickets in an Australia season.

ABOVE   South Africans Graeme Pollock
(left) and Eddie Barlow (right) relax at their
motel pool after their undefeated stand of
225 for the third wicket against Australia at
the end of day two, in the Fourth Test at
Adelaide in the 1963/64 summer. They were
finally parted the following day, having accumulated 341in a record-breaking partnership.
Match Scores: Australia 345 (P.J.Burge 91,
R.B.Simpson 78, B.K.Shepherd 70, B.C.Booth
58, T.L.Goddard 5 for 60) and 331
(B.K.Shepherd 78, N.C.O'Neill 66); South
Africa 595 (E.J.Barlow 201, R.G.Pollock 175,
N.J.N.Hawke 6 for 139) and 82 for 0. South
Africa won by 10 wickets.

RIGHT Colin Cowdrey is dismissed, caught Grout bowled Walters for 79 in England's first innings of the Fifth Test of the 1965/66 series at Melbourne. Match Scores: England 485 for 9 dec (K.F.Barrington 115, J.M.Parks 89, J.H.Edrich 85, M.C.Cowdrey 79, F.J.Titmus 42, K.D.Walters 4 for 53) and 69 for 3; Australia 543 for 8 dec (R.M.Cowper 307, W.M.Lawry 108, K.D.Walters 60). Match drawn.

BELOW Sir Garfield Sobers — 'The greatest batsman I've seen' said Australian cricketer Norman O'Neill. All his grace, power and timing are captured in this superb cover-drive off Richie Benaud in a game for South Australia against New South Wales at the SCG in 1964. The wicketkeeper is Doug Ford, seen watching the ball race again to the boundary during Sobers innings of 138.

Sir Garfield Sobers — 'The greatest batsman I've seen' said Australian cricketer Norman O'Neill.

ABOVE The old Pressbox at the SCG, which was then a vast, glassed-in affair far superior in comfort and the view it gave of play to most English boxes of the period. However, while grounds and spectator comfort has come a long way since these days of the 1960s, still the commentators conditions in certain grounds are far from ideal.

BELOW LEFT Barry Jarman, who deputized for Wally Grout in many Tests, played in 19 Tests from 1959 to 1969. His record behind the stumps was 50 catches and 4 stumpings. He managed two half centuries in his Test career, scoring 400 runs at an average of 14.81.

RIGHT Openers Bill Lawry and Bob Simpson head out to the wicket in the Fourth Test at Old Trafford in 1964, in what would be a record opening stand of 201, breaking the 1909 record of Bardsley and Gregory who had put on 180 for the first wicket at the Oval. This was Simpson's first Test century in this his 30th Test match, and was the longest innings ever played against England (12 hours 42 minutes). Match Scores: Australia 656 for 8 dec (R.B.Simpson 311, W.M.Lawry 106, B.C.Booth 98, N.C.O'Neill 47) and 4 for 0; England 611 (K.F.Barrington 256, E.R.Dexter 174, J.M.Parks 60, G.Boycott 58, G.D.McKenzie 7 for 153). Match drawn.

BELOW The Sheridan Stand (centre) and part of the Brewongle Stand at the Sydney Cricket Ground in 1962. Rain delays have always been the scurge of all cricket lovers and no doubt will continue like that as long as cricket is played.

ABOVE TOP Bob Simpson applauds as Victorian Ian Redpath dives full-length to catch David Allen at Lord's in May, 1964 against the MCC. This however was not indicative of the standard of catching and fielding on this tour, which was below the usual high standards the Australians set.

ABOVE MIDDLE Ian Redpath blasts the winning run in the Ashes-deciding Third Test at Headingley, Leeds, in 1964. Peter Burge set up this win with a great innings. Match

Scores: England 268 (J.M.Parks 68, E.R.Dexter 66, N.J.N.Hawke 5 for 75, G.D.McKenzie 4 for 74) and 229 (K.F.Barrington 85); Australia 389 (P.J.P.Burge 160, W.M.Lawry 78, F.J.Titmus 4 for 69) and 111 for 3 (I.R.Redpath 58). Australia won by 7 wickets.

ABOVE BOTTOM Australian fieldsmen crowd in around England's tailender Norman Gifford as he dabs at Tom Veivers at Lord's in the Second Test in 1964. Vievers, while a good off-spin bowler, capturing 33 wickets at 41.66, he was also a spectacular but inconsistent batsman, scoring 813 runs at an average of 31.26, with a top score of 88.

... many had said the tourists of 1964 were the worst team ever to leave our shores...

TOP Bob Simpson, whose hard-headed captaincy proved vital in 1964 in England, hits a four against the MCC at Lord's. Many had said the tourists of 1964 were the worst team ever to leave our shores, with the retirements of Benaud, Harvey, Davidson and Mackay. However, the critics were proved wrong yet again, when the Australians retained the Ashes with a 1-0 series win.

BOTTOM Bob Simpson and the loneliness of command. Answering sports-writers questions in the sheds at the end of a days play. His association with the game would last over four decades, as a player (both batsman and bowler), captain, coach and commentator. He retired from the Test arena in 1967/68 at age 32, however was coaxed out of retiremtent at age 41 to lead a team of raw recruits when the World Series cricket revolution turned the cricket world upside down. His full Test career was 62 Tests, scoing 4869 runs at an average of 46.81, with a top score of 311. He also took 71 wickets at 42.26 bowling leg-spin.

ABOVE The Australian Eleven for the First Test at Brisbane in the Ashes series of 1965–66. This game was notable for the Test debut of Doug Walters (middle row, far left). He scored 155 in his only innings in this match and 410 at 68.33 for his first series. He would go on to play in 74 Tests, scoring 5357 runs at 48.26, with a high score of 250 (against New Zealand in Christchurch in 1977).

LEFT England's D.J.Brown, who captured 5 for 63 in Australia's first innings of the Third Test at the SCG in 1966, bowls one down to Doug Walters. And while Walters remained 35 not out, Brown earlier had captured three wickets in one over to make the follow-on almost certain for Australia. Match Scores: England 488 (R.W.Barber 185, J.H.Edrich 103, G.Boycott 84, D.A.Allen 50, N.J.N.Hawke 7 for 105); Australia 221 (R.M.Cowper 60, G.Thomas 51, D.G.Brown 5 for 63) and 174 (F.J.Titmus 4 for 40, D.A.Allen 4 for 47). England won by an innings and 93 runs.

BELOW Australia's Peter Burge (left) has a drink with England's John Murray after England's victory in the Third Test at the Sydney Cricket Ground.

OPPOSITE West Indian great fast-bowler Wesley Hall showing some aspiring bowlers how to bowl at Coogee in Sydney's eastern suburbs in October, 1965, while in Sydney with the Queensland Sheffield Shield team.

ABOVE West Indian, Charlie Griffith, who played Test cricket from 1960 to 1969, was a tearawy fast bowler, who formed a lethal partnership with the great Wess Hall. In his 28 Tests he captured 94 wickets at an average of 28.54, with a best return of 6 for 36 in the fourth Test against England at Headingley. In a controversial career there were some who doubted the validity of his bowling action at various times.

ABOVE LEFT Brian Booth (Australia) and Mike Smith (England) tossing up before the Third Test of the 1965/66 series in Sydney. The series ended 1-all, with England winning this Test, while Australia was successful in the Fourth Test in Adelaide. Booth had stood in for the injured Australian captain Bob Simpson in both this and the First Test. Brian Booth played in 29 Tests between 1961 and 1966, scored 1,773 runs at an average of 42.21, with a top score of 169.

ABOVE RIGHT Bill Lawry watches, hand on hip, as Mike Smith (white hat) knocks the bails off with Peter Burge hopelessly out of his ground in the Third Test of the 1965/66 Ashes series in Sydney.

OPPOSITE RIGHT Budding fast bowler Dennis Lillee, 18, pictured at the WACA Ground, Perth on 20th December, 1967 — the day he was selected in the Western Australian Colts team. At right is the teams opening batsman, David Bull. Even at the tender age of 18, Lillee had that steely determination in his eye.

Keith Stackpole was one of the real entertainers of post-war cricket — he liked to attack from the very first ball.

ABOVE Keith Stackpole, one of the real entertainers of post-war cricket, liked to attack from the very first ball. Originally a middle-order batsman, and part time leg-spin bowler, he graduated to become an opener who loved the hook shot. Stackpole retired at the end of the New Zealand tour in 1974, primarily because of the treatment of Test players by the Australian Board Of Control. He subsequently wrote a book 'Off My Chest', in which can now be seen years later as a warning to the authorities about what eventually transpired with World Series Cricket. He played in 43 Tests from 1965 and 1974, scoring 2,807 runs at an average of 37.42, with a high score of 207.

OPPOSITE TOP Bill Lawry and Ashley Mallett (both on left) stand in silence at the Oval before the start of the fourth days play in the Fifth and final Test, 1968. They stood for one minute in silence in tribute to the famous Australian batsman Stanley Joseph McCabe, who had died, aged 58, in the garden of his home at Beauty Point on Sydney Harbour the day before.

OPPOSITE BOTTOM The West Indies Garfield Sobers reaches his century by cover driving Corling for 3 at the Sydney Cricket Ground in November, 1968. He was eventually dismissed for 130, caught Taber, bowled Renneberg.

Third days play West Indies v Western Australia in October, 1968. It's only a split second after the ball has snicked the bat, but already Western Australian vice-captain John Inverarity must fear the worst. Wicketkeeper Jackie Hendricks is moving into position to take the catch off big Wesley Hall's bowling. This was the opening match of the 1968/69 tour, with the West Indies winning the match by 6 wickets.

Indian captain M.A.K.Pataudi on drives his counterpart Bob Simpson in
the Fourth Test at the Sydney Cricket Ground in the summer of 1967/68.
standing in slips is Ian Chappell, with Brian Taber the wicketkeeper.
Match Scores: Australia 317 (K.D.Walters 94, A.P.Sheahan 72,
D.M.Lawry 66) and 292 (R.M.Cowper 165, W.M.Lawry 52,
E.A.S.Prasanna 4 for 96); Inda 268 (S.Abid Ali 78, M.A.K.Pataudi 51,
E.W.Freeman 4 for 86) and 197 (S.Abid Ali 81, R.B.Simpson 5 for 59,
R.M.Cowper 4 for 49). Australia won by 144 runs.

Sir Donald Bradman raises the flag during the Australia Day ceremony at Adelaide Oval before play in the Fourth Test between Australia and the West Indies from January 24–29, 1969. Watching are team captains Garfield Sobers (left) and Bill Lawry, with both sides lined up behind.

OPPOSITE Garfield Sobers off drives spinner John Gleeson for four to reach his century in the Fifth Test at the Sydney Cricket Ground in February, 1969. The effort of Doug Walters in this Test (who became the first player to ever score a double century and a century in each innings of a Test match) can not be understated. In this series he batted in just six innings, scoring four centuries and two half-centuries, with an aggregate of 699 runs at a healthy average of 116.5. Not too bad for the boy from Dungog. While Australia's win in this Test match won them the series 3–1, it was their captain Bill Lawry's decision to set the West Indies the ridiculous target of 735 to win that has scribes nearly 40 years later still scratching their heads. Match Scores: Australia 619 (K.D.Walters 242, W.M.Lawry 151, E.W.Freeman 56) and 394 for 8 dec (I.R.Redpath 132, K.D.Walters 103); West Indies 279 (M.C.Carew 64, C.H.Lloyd 53, A.N.Connolly 4 for 61) and 352 (S.M.Nurse 137, G.S.Sobers 113). Australia won by 382 runs.

ABOVE Wes Hall, who played grade cricket in Queensland during 1965, is a fearsome sight as he releases a thunderbolt. It was a time when Test players were more than happy to do 'their bit' for the local suburban teams.

ABOVE West Indian batsman, Clive Lloyd, ducks a bumper from Australia's Grahan McKenzie in the Fourth Test at Adelaide Oval, 1969. Match Scores: West Indies 276 (G.S.Sobers 110, B.F.Butcher 52, E.W.Freeman 4 for 52) and 616 (B.F.Butcher 118, M.C.Carew 90, R.Kanhai 80, D.A.J.Holdford 80, G.S.Sobers 52, A.N.Connolly 5 for 122); Australia 533 (K.D.Walters 110, I.M.Chappell 76, W.M.Lawry 62, K.R.Stackpole 62, G.D.McKenzie 59, A.P.Sheahan 51, L.R.Gibbs 4 for 145) and 339 for 9 (I.M.Chappell 96, W.M.Lawry 89, K.R.Stackpole 50, K.D.Walters 50). Match drawn.

OPPOSITE TOP After the conclusion of the Fifth Test, in Sydney, the Frank Worrell trophy was presented by the West Indies skipper Gary Sobers to the victorious Australian team, skippered by Bill Lawry. On the left can be seen two of the youngsters in Australia's team that day, Brian Taber and Paul Sheahan.

OPPOSITE BOTTOM South Australian Test batsman, Ian Chappell, is congratulated by his grandfather and famous international, Victor Richardson, after being named Cricketer of the year for 1969.

Greg and Ian Chappell, two Australian cricket captains, brothers, great batsmen, and leaders. The two grandsons of Victor Richardson stood tall, one mainly for his captaincy and the other mainly for his batsmanship. The Australian team needed an Ian Chappell when he was appointed captain in the Seventh Test of the 1970/71 series against England. He turned the team around to begin a successful period in Australian cricket, leading Australia in 30 Tests, winning 15, drawing 10 and losing only 5. Apart from losing his first Test as captain against Ray Illingworth's 1970/71 team, Ian Chappell never lost a series as captain. His full record is: 1971/72 v England lost 0–1; 1972 v England won 2, lost 2, drew 1; 1972/73 v Pakistan won 3–0; 1973 v West Indies won 2, drew 3; 1973/74

1974/75 v England won 4, lost 1, drew 1; 1975 v England won 1, drew 3. Greg Chappell, while also a very good leader, will probably be remembered more for his elegant strokeplay and his massive accumulation of runs. He played 87 Tests from 1970/71 to 1983/84, scoring 7110 runs at an average of 53.86, with a high score of 247 runs. He scored 24 centuries and 31 half-centuries and scored a hundred on debut (108 v England at Perth in the Second Test) and another hundred in his last Test (182 v Pakistan at Sydney in the Fifth Test). In a unique achievement he also scored a century in each innings in his debut as captain (123 and 109 not out v West Indies at Sydney in the First Test on 1975/76). He captained his country in 48 Tests, for 21 wins, 14 draws and

1970 – 1977

7

1970

THE 1970S WAS A TUMULTUOUS DECADE in Australian Cricket, with the most far-reaching changes in a hundred years of international competition engulfing the game in 1977. Few of the major players in that cricket revolution whose careers were just getting underway as the decade commenced — especially batsmen Greg Chappell, the younger brother of Ian Chappell (who would assume the Australian Test captaincy from the veteran Bill Lawry in 1971) and the West Australian pair, wicketkeeper Rod Marsh and speed bowler Dennis Lillee — could have envisaged the revolution that the 1970s would be. None of us could.

Fiery pace bowler John Snow (31 wickets for the series) scuttled the Australians

The decade opened with the last tour of South Africa by an Australian team for more than two decades. In the final months of 1969 Australia had defeated India in India, no easy feat in any era, before travelling to South Africa in January 1970. The Proteas dominated the four-test series, 4–0, and were keen to play a fifth Test but the Australian Board of Control refused the request put forward by their hosts to contribute $200 per man of the proposed $500 player payment. Graham Pollock's 274 in the second Test at Durban was described as one of the finest knocks ever played against an Australia team. But political and sporting sanctions against the South African government's apartheid policies would mean a generation of Australians — and great South African players — would not see the likes of such an innings for some time.

In the summer of 1970–71, Ray Illingworth's England team travelled to Australia and recaptured the Ashes for the first time since 1956. Fiery pace bowler John Snow (31 wickets for the series) scuttled the Australians and although the third Test in Melbourne was abandoned due to rain and replaced with an historic seventh match, the series — and the Ashes — were ultimately lost, 2–0. Bill Lawry was sensationally sacked by the Australian selectors for the historic seventh Test, which was played in Sydney, and the match reached flashpoint when arguments between Illingworth and the umpires led to a walk-off by the England team. Snow, who had been warned for intimidatory bowling, had been grabbed by a spectator on the boundary and Illingworth had had enough. With the likelihood of a forfeit becoming an ever-increasing reality, England returned to the field and promptly won the match.

In January, 1971, the first one-day international match was played in Australia. The 40 over a side game was hastily organised for Victorian cricket fans after the traditional Boxing Day match was washed out. A domestic one-day competition had been held the previous year and England had been holding such matches since 1963 but the new form of the game attracted 46,000 fans to the MCG which produced a healthy gate of $33,984. For the record, England scored 190 from 39.4 eight ball overs with Australia gathering in the total in the 35th over. The success of the one-day game with Australia fans set officials discussing the possibility of a World Cup competition along the lines of the limited over format but it would be another four years before the idea got off the ground.

Sobers' 254 at the MCG was acknowledged by Sir Donald Bradman as arguably the best innings ever seen in Australia.

Later that year the Australian Board of Control cancelled the proposed South African Tour of Australia, largely due to series of violent protests during the South African rugby tour, and in spite of the South African Cricket Associations strong condemnation of its government's actions. However, mindful of public opinion and realising that a tour by a South African team would become a flashpoint for protests, the Board conducted a series against a World XI'. In November 1971, players of the calibre of Garfield Sobers and Clive Lloyd (West Indies), Graeme and Peter Pollock (South Africa) and Tony Greig (England) joined players from the sub-continent to play a series of international 'tests' against Australia. Sobers' 254 at the MCG (2 sixes, 33 fours in 376 minutes) was acknowledged by Sir Donald Bradman as arguably the best innings ever seen in Australia. High praise indeed. However, there were Australian success stories in that series as well. Ian Chappell scored four centuries and Dennis Lillee established his reputation as a world class bowler.

In 1972 Ian Chappell led a young Australian team to England in search of Ashes glory. England captured the first Test at Old Trafford but the second match of the series, played at Lords, will be forever known as 'Massie's Match'. The West Australian bowler captured an Australian record 16 wickets for the match with figures of 8/84 and 8/53 to set up Australia's eight wicket victory. Although England won the Fourth Test to retain the Ashes, Australia's Fifth Test victory at The Oval squared the series two Tests-all and augured well for the future. Lillee and Marsh — a combination that would keep Australia in good stead

1977

1970

during the next decade — dominated the match, with Lillee's ten-wicket haul bringing his series total to a record 31 wickets. Marsh contributed 23 dismissals in the series, which was also a record. Record takings, increased sponsorship and the consolidation of the one-day game with the playing of the 'Prudential Trophy' were other highlights of a test series that would have far-reaching implications for the course of Australian cricket during the remainder of the decade.

Lillee and Thompson almost single-handedly brought an end to the playing career of England captain Mike Denness.

Australia defeated Pakistan 3–0 in the summer of 1972–73 before embarking on a five-Test tour of the West Indies. The series opened disastrously when Dennis Lillee suffered a career-threatening back injury in the first Test but under the aggressive, uncompromising captaincy of Ian Chappell, Australia ground out a 2–0 series win. Chappell's charges returned to Australia undefeated in the 12-match tour and could arguably lay claim to being the best team in the world. But Ashes success still beckoned and the team would surely be tested in the first World Cup tournament which was scheduled for the Northern Hemisphere summer of 1975.

After a three-Test series win against New Zealand in the summer of 1973–74, Australia toured New Zealand in March with a dawn series (1–1). The Chappell brothers plundered runs in New Zealand but the home-team recorded a sobering win in the second Test, largely due to the good from of Richard Hadlee (3/59 and 4/71) with the ball and Glen Turner (101 and 110) with the bat. Whilst on tour in Australia, New Zealand took part in the domestic 'Gillette Cup' one-day knockout competition but was beaten by Western Australia in the final in February, 1974.

In the Australian summer of 1974–75, the return of Dennis Lillee, and the emergence of his pace bowling partner Jeff Thompson, became the spearhead in Ian Chappell's Ashes quest. In the emphatic 4-1 Test victory, Lillee and Thompson almost single-handedly brought an end to the playing career of England captain Mike Denness. Facing a series loss, Denness dropped himself for the Fourth Test, because of poor form and John Edrich led England in the match. Ian Redpath (105) and Greg Chappell (144) set up an early declaration and the bowlers — Lillee, Thomson, Max Walker and Ashley Mallet — did the rest. Denness returned for the final two Tests of the series but the Ashes were lost.

When Australia lost the sixth Test of the series, played at the MCG in February, Australian captain Ian Chappell lamented, somewhat pointedly, that the Board would 'probably knock back our bonus now we lost' despite the 4-1 series win. Money would continue to be a major issue but few could foresee that the one-day game may be the answer. Four years after the first international one-day match was played at the MCG, England defeated Australia by three wickets in front of a not-so inspiring crowd of 18, 837. Not surprisingly, the Chappell brothers, Ian and Greg, top-scored with 42 and 44 runs respectively.

vandals sabotaged the Headingly pitch when Australia was poised for victory in the vital third Test of the series

In June 1975 Australia took part in the inaugural World Cup competition which was staged in England before the Ashes Test series. Australia defeated Pakistan and Sri Lanka in the preliminary rounds before falling to the West Indies in the last match before the semi-finals. Drawn to play England at Headingly, Australian all-rounder Gary Gilmour took 6/14 as the home nation crumbled to be all out for 93. However, it was a different story in the final against the West Indies, with their big-hitting batsmen scoring 291 off 60 overs. Australia fell 17 runs short but inside the final seven overs, the mark still looked within reach of the last of the Australians unlikely batting heroes Lillee and Thompson. The match, in which Clive Lloyd scored 102, and five Australians were run-out, was a marathon … official speeches finished in twilight at 9:00 pm, English daylight-saving time.

The Ashes series against England was no less exciting. Mike Denness effectively offered his resignation as England captain when he won the toss at Edgbaston and offered Australia a bat. After the innings and 85 run loss, Denness was replaced by 29-year-old, former South African national Tony Greig, the captain of Sussex. England fared better in the second Test and after the drawn Test, vandals sabotaged the Headingly pitch when Australia was poised for victory in the vital third Test of the series. With England forced to follow on in the Fourth Test (and added 538 to its first innings total of 191 in response to Australia's declaration of 9/532) the match wound down into an inevitable draw and Australia retained the Ashes, 1–0. But Australian sporting fans had a target … the unflappable England captain Tony Greig, who would play a major role in the revolution that was soon to overtake the game.

1977

TOP: South African Eddie Barlow was one of the most popular players of the 1960s and '70s. A strong opening batsman and an aggressive medium paced bowler, plus a brilliant 'slipper', he like many of his era were an enormous loss to International cricket, with their expulsion in the 1970s. He played just 30 Tests, scored 2516 runs at an average of 45.74 and took 40 wickets at 34.04.

BOTTOM: Mike Proctor was another of the victims of South Africa's Test 'ban', who in his only two series (both against Australia) took 41 wickets at an average of 15.02 in only seven Tests. His bowling action was very similar to Australia's Max Walker, if not bowling off the wrong foot, at the very least looking most awkward. Either way it was very effective.

The classic off-break action of England off-spinner and Captain, Ray Illingworth. Illingworth played 61 Tests from 1958 to 1973, scoring 1,836 runs at an average of 23.24, with a high score of 113, and took 122 wickets at 31.2 with a best return of 6 for 29. He captained England in 31 Tests, winning 12, losing 5 and drawing 14. While being widely regarded as an excellent captain, his batting and bowling efforts were much better than people gave him credit for. A good example of his abilities under pressure was in the Seventh and Ashes deciding Test, when Australia required just 223 for victory to draw the series and retain the Ashes. John Snow, their leading wicket-taker, had been injured trying to catch a Keith Stackpole hook shot and was unfit to bowl, but Illingworth put himself on and broke the back of the top-order, removing Stackpole, Redpath and Greg Chappell.

While being widely regarded as an excellent captain, Ray Illingworth's batting and bowling efforts were much better than people gave him credit for.

World XI captain Gary Sobers disguises his bowling hand as he runs to the crease at the practice nets in Brisbane. Other members of the team are doing exercises in the background. Sobers was quite at home bowling fast-medium pace or off-spin, both with equal effect.

ABOVE Sir Robert Menzies, in February 1971 with former English player and captain Mr. Frank Woolley (left), who like his fellow countryman, Jack Hobbs, played Test cricket over decades rather than years (1909-1934), and Bert Oldfield (right), a popular fixture in the Australian teams from the end of World War 1 up to the late 1930s.

RIGHT Ian Chappell is mobbed in the Fifth Test against England at Melbourne, after he reached his century. Match Scores: Australia 493 for 9 dec (I.M.Chappell 111, R.W.Marsh 92, I.R.Redpath 72, W.M.Lawry 56, K.D.Walters 55) and 169 for 4 dec (W.M.Lawry 42); England 392 (B.L.D'Oliveira 117, B.W.Luckhurst 109, R.Illingworth 41) and 161 for 0 (G.Boycott 76, J.H.Edrich 74). Match drawn.

LEFT Ray Illingworth, clean bowled by Dennis Lillee for 24 in England's first innings of the Sixth Test in the series of 1970/71 at Adelaide. This was Lillee's first Test match for Australia, taking five on debut. Match Scores: England 470 (J.H.Edrich 130, K.W.R.Fletcher 80, G.Boycott 58, J.H.Hampshire 55, B.L.D'Oliveira 47, D.K.Lillee 5 for 84) and 233 for 4 dec (G.Boycott 119, R.Illingworth 48, J.H.Edrich 40); Australia 235 (K.R.Stackpole 87, P.Lever 4 for 49) and 328 for 3 (K.R.Stackpole 136, I.M.Chappell 104). Match drawn.

BELOW John Snow hits the fence with his hand, breaking his forefinger, after unsuccessfully trying to catch a Keith Stackpole hook shot at the Sydney Cricket Ground in the Seventh Test in 1971.

RIGHT John Snow is grabbed by a spectator who had consumed far too much alcohol, in front of the Paddington Hill at the SCG during the Seventh and deciding Test of the 1970/71 series. In a sensational aftermarth to a series of events, which included Jenner retiring hurt, Snow's altercation with a spectator and finally a rain of beer cans onto the field, Ray Illingworth firstly sat down with his team on the field and then lead them off back to their dressing rooms. When threatened with the possibility of losing the match by forfeit, he wisely decided to return to the field. This series saw the Ashes return to England, after a 2–0 series win, with Ray Illingworth becoming their first captain since Douglas Jardine, 38 years earlier to recapture the Ashes in Australia. Match Scores: England 184 (R.Illingworth 42) and 302 (B.W.Luckhurst 59, J.H.Edrich 57, B.L.D'Oliveira 47); Australia 264 (G.S.Chappell 65, I.R.Redpath 59, K.D.Walters 42) and 160 (K.R.Stackpole 67). England won by 62 runs.

LEFT England captain Ray Illingworth and his number one strike bowler, John Snow, argue with umpire Lou Rowan after Australian lower-order batsman Terry Jenner retired after he was hit in the head by a lifting ball from paceman Snow, during the Seventh Test in 1971.

LEFT South African Test star batsman Barry Richards pushes a ball through mid-wicket during his century for South Australia against New South Wales at the Sydney Cricket Ground in 1971. Richard was one of the great losses to Test cricket, because of the embargo placed by the other playing cricket nations. The Australian public were fortunate however to see him play Sheffield Shield for South Australia during 1970–71, when he scored 1538 runs at an average of 109.86, including a career high of 356 (325 of which were scored in one day). In only 4 Tests (all against Australia) he scored 508 runs at an average of 72.57, with 2 centuries, including a high score of 140. Old time South African supporters will never forget the Second Test at Durban, when Richards (140) and Graeme Pollock (274) slaughtered the Australian attack. Match Scores: South Africa 622 for 9 dec (R.G.Pollock 274, B.A.Richards 140, H.R.Lance 61); Australia 157 (A.P.Sheahan 62) and 336 (I.R.Redpath 74, K.D.Walters 74, K.R.Stackpole 71). South Africa won by an innings and 129 runs.

RIGHT Dennis Lillee, was a bank teller in 1970 — a far cry from the bowler world batsmen would come to fear most, in just two short years.

OPPOSITE The MCC versus The Australians at Lords, May, 1972. Ray Illingworth (MCC) is out lbw off Ashley Mallett for one. Ian Chappell is at silly mid-off, Keith Stackpole at slip and Rod Marsh the wicketkeeper.

ABOVE No finer example of a cover drive than this one perfectly executed by Gary Sobers, who is regarded as the greatest all-rounder in Test history. This image shows Sobers batting for the Rest of the World against Australia in the Third Test (these matches comprised an unofficial Test series) at the MCG on January 5, 1972. Sobers, the Rest of the World captain elegantly drives a ball from Terry Jenner to the boundary through the covers to bring up his double century, in one of his many great innings. This tour was organized as a replacement for the scheduled tour by the South African team to Australia that summer, which had been cancelled by the Australian Board of Control. Match Scores: World X1 184 (A.W.Greig 66, D.K.Lillee 5 for 48) and 514 (G.S.Sobers 254, Z.Abbas 86, T.J.Jenner 4 for 87); Australia 285 (G.S.Chappell 115, A.W.Greig 4 for 41) and 317 (K.D.Walters 127, B.Bedi 4 for 81). World X1 won by 97 runs.

ABOVE LEFT Before the start of play on the third day of the Fifth Test, 1972, between Australia and England. Ian Chappell (Left) was preparing to resume batting, hence the bat and gloves. Both made centuries in Australia's first innings. Match Scores: England 284 (A.P.E.Knott 92, P.H.Parfitt 51, J.H.Hampshire 42, D.K.Lillee 5 for 58) and 356 (B.Wood 90, A.P.E.Knott 63, B.L.D'Oliveira 43, D.K.Lillee 5 for 123); Australia 399 (I.M.Chappell 118, G.S.Chappell 113, R.Edwards 79, D.L.Underwood 4 for 90) and 242 for 5 (K.R.Stackpole 79, A.P.Sheahan 44, R.W.Marsh 43). Australia won by 5 wickets.

ABOVE RIGHT Ian Chappell hooks Intikhab for four in the first Test at Adelaide. Match Scores: Pakistan 257 (Wasim Bari 72, Intikihab Alam 64, D.K.Lillee 4 for 49, R.A.Massie 4 for 70) and 214 (Sadiq Mohammad 81, A.A.Mallett 8 for 59); Australia 585 (I.M.Chappell 196, R.W.Marsh 118, R.Edwards 89). Australia won by an innings and 114 runs.

RIGHT Greg Chappell also gives Intikhab Alam the treatment, scoring a four in the same game.

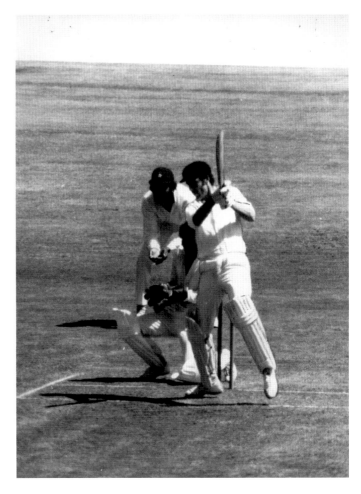

OPPOSITE Sir Garfield St Auburn Sobers played for the West Indies from 1954 to 1974 in 93 Tests, scoring 8032 runs at an average of 57.78, with 26 centuries, a top score of 365 not out, took 109 catches, captured 235 wickets at an average of 34.03, with a best of 6 for 73. He also captained the West Indies in 39 Tests. One of the true greats in any era of the game.

ABOVE Greg Chappell comes off the Sydney Cricket Ground on 107 not out, during the Fourth International against the World X1 in January, 1972. Earlier his brother Ian had scored 119. Match Scores: Australia 312 (K.R.Stackpole 104, R.W.Marsh 77, J.Benaud 54, B.Bedi 4 for 85) and 546 (G.S.Chappell 197, I.M.Chappell 119, K.R.Stackpole 95, K.J.O'Keeffe 54, Intikhab Alam 4 for 132); World X1 277 (Intikhab Alam 73, A.W.Greig 70, R.A.Massie 7 for 76) and 173 for 5 (H.M.Ackerman 87, S.M.Gavaskar 68, K.O'Keeffe 3 for 34). Match drawn.

Sir Garfield St Auburn Sobers,
one of the true greats
in any era of the game.

OPPOSITE Sir Richard Hadlee, in 1973, at the beginning of a long and distinguished career. He was by far and away the best bowler New Zealand cricket has produced. His father, Walter, also player Test cricket for New Zealand, playing 11 Tests from 1937 to 1951. Richard Hadlee played 86 Tests from 1973 to 1990, took 431 wickets at an average of 22.29 (first player to pass 400 Test wickets), with a best of 9 for 52 (v Australia). He also scored 3124 runs at an average of 27.16, with a high score of 151.

TOP After the Second Test in Sydney during the summer of 1974/75, Australia's captain Ian Chappell (right) could be saying to New Zealand's skipper Bevan Congdon, 'Well we got out of that one okay', after the match was officially abandoned because of heavy rain which had saturated the Sydney Cricket Ground. A win here would have given the New Zealander's their first win ever in a Test match on Australian shores. Match Scores: New Zealand 312 (J.M.Parker 108, K.J.Wadsworth 54, K.D.Walters 4 for 39) and 305 for 9 dec (J.F.M.Morrisson 117, B.F.Hastings 83); Australia 162 (R.J.Hadlee 4 for 33) and 30 for 2. Match drawn.

BOTTOM Decked out in their best 70s gear, Captain Ian Chappell lends a hand to fellow touring selector and batsman Doug Walters before the 14 man team flew out of Sydney for the second leg of the series against New Zealand in February, 1974. The series in Australia was won 2–0 by the Australians, while the New Zealand leg was drawn 1–all.

LEFT TOP Vivian Richards (in hat) runs to embrace bowler Michael Holding, who had Gary Gilmour caught by Alvin Kallicharran for a duck in the New South Wales versus West Indies game at the Sydney Cricket Ground in November, 1975.

LEFT BOTTOM Vivian Richards plays at a Dave Colley delivery for the West Indies against New South Wales in November, 1975. Match Scores: West Indies 270 (A.I.Kallicharran 78, M.A.Holding 62, G.J.Gilmour 3 for 58) and 200 (D.L.Murray 46, D.Colley 5 for 72); New South Wales 272 for 6 dec (A.Turner 106, R.B.McCosker 46, A.Roberts 2 for 55) and 146 (A.Turner 66, M.A.Holding 6 for 60). West Indies won by 52 runs.

Bowler Michael Holding had Gary Gilmour caught by Alvin Kallicharran for a duck in the New South Wales versus West Indies game

ABOVE Rodney Marsh takes a Lillee delivery, with Vivian Richards the batsman, Fifth Test between Australia and the West Indies at Adelaide in January, 1976. Match Scores: Australia 418 (I.R.Redpath 103, G.J.Gilmour 95, V.A.Holder 5 for 108) and 345 for 7 dec (A.Turner 136, I.R.Redpath 65); West indies 274 (K.D.Boyce 95, A.I.Kallicharran 76, J.R.Thomson 4 for 68) and 299 (I.V.A.Richards 101, K.D.Boyce 69, A.I.Kallicharran 67). Australia won by 190 runs.

ABOVE Bishen Bedi, playing for India in 1976. He toured Australia three times, twice for India (in 1967/68 and 1977/78) and once with the World X1 (in 1971/72) and was a real crowd favourite with his colourful turbans. He was a naturally talented slow left-arm orthodox bowler who conjured wonderful variations in flight, loop, spin and pace. He played cricket for India in 67 Tests from 1966 to 1979, took 266 wickets at an average of 28.71, with a best of 7 for 98.

Bishen Bedi was a naturally talented slow left-arm orthodox bowler who conjured wonderful variations in flight, loop, spin and pace.

RIGHT TOP The famous Melbourne Cricket Ground scoreboard during the 100th Test celebration in Match, 1977. The score shows Australia 3 for 27 before lunch on the first day, and worst was to come, when they were all out for 138. By days end England were in a handy position at 1 for 29 in reply. But the following day the great Dennis Lillee destroyed the English batting lineup, capturing 6 for 26 to see them dismissed for an even lower score of 95. Lillee once again had righted the ship for Australia to set them on course for a famous victory.

RIGHT BOTTOM Greg Chappell and Jack Ryder, who at 87 was the oldest of the veterans present at the Centenary Test at Melbourne in March 1977. In celebration of the 100th birthday of England versus Australia Test cricket matches, and in a wonderfully organised occasion, almost 200 former Test cricketers attended what turned out to be a supreme contest worthy of the occasion. Match Scores: Australia 138 (G.S,Chappell 40) and 419 for 9 dec (R.W.Marsh 110, I.C.Davis 68, K.D.Walters 66. D.W.Hookes 56, C.M.Old 4 for 104); England 95 (D.K.Lillee 6 for 26, M.H.N.Walker 4 for 54) and 417 (D.W.Randall 174, D.L.Amiss 65, J.M.Brealey 43, A.P.E.Knott 42, A.W.Greig 41, D.K.Lillee 5 for 139).Australia won by 45 runs, incredibly the same result as the very First Test, when Australia also won by 45 runs at Melbourne way back in 1877.

ABOVE Australian great Doug Walters shows his son how to grip the bat during the 1970s. 'Dougie' was one of the real characters of the game, be it his brilliant strokeplay, his uncanny ability to break partnerships with his innocuous medium pace deliveries or his apparent laid-back approach to the game. The chant for Walters would often reverberate at his home ground of the SCG.

OPPOSITE Andy Roberts played 47 Tests for the West Indies from 1974 to 1983, took 202 wickets at an average of 25.61, with a career best of 7 for 54. Roberts was the first in a long line of pace bowlers produced by the West Indies from the mid 1970s for the next 20 years. He was not your 'normal' fast bowler, with no apparent emotion, but his deliveries had plenty of 'emotion' behind them. His bouncer was dangerously accurate, and came through at a range of speeds and angles.

'Dougie' was one of the real characters of the game

ABOVE Jeff Thompson, played for Australia in 51 Tests from 1972–73 to 1985, captured 200 wickets at 28.0 and was one of the fastest ever bowlers to play Test cricket. His unusual slinging action generated enormous pace and confounded many batsman because the ball was out of sight for much of the delivery. His 'sand-shoe crusher' claimed many a victim, both in wickets and toes. After a disappointing debut against Pakistan in 1972–73, hampered by injury, he was recalled for the battle against Mike Denness' English side of 1974–75, taking 33 wickets, destroying both the body and the mind of many an English batsman.

OPPOSITE Joel Garner, who started his Test career in 1977, was one of many great West Indian fast bowlers that destroyed many opposing batting line-ups. At 6ft 8ins, his deliveries would always rear up from a good length to cause untold discomfort to the very best batsman. Added to this was his expert use of the yorker. He played 58 Tests for the West Indies, took 259 wickets at just 20.97, with a best return of 6 for 56.

Michael Holding had possibly the most graceful bowling approach of any fast bowler, which belied the 'whispering death' tag that was given him because of his sheer speed of delivery.

ABOVE Dennis Lillee, played 70 Tests from 1970–71 to 1984, taking 355 wickets at 23.92, with a career best of 7 for 83 against the West Indies in 1981. In first-class matches he took 882 wickets at 23.46 from 1969–70 to 1988, with a career best of 8 for 29 against a World X1 in 1971–72. He was the complete bowler, who delivered the ball at frightening pace and could always be relied upon to bowl one more over. After capturing 31 Test wickets during the 1972 Ashes tour, Lillee broke down with spinal stree fractures the next year. Fully recovered, he teamed up with Jeff Thomson in the 1974–75 series against England to form a brilliant two pronged attack. While in the 1977 Centenary Test, Lillee was brilliant capturing 6 for 26 and 5 for 139 to get Australia home by 45 runs. The young tearaway of 1971 had become possibly the greatest fast-bowler his country had produced by the end of a wonderful career 18 years later.

LEFT Rodney Marsh, who played 96 Tests for Australia from 1970/71 to 1984, took 343 catches and 12 stumpings and scored 3,633 runs at an average of 26.51, with a high score of 132. When first selected for Australia in the First Test against Ray Illingworth's team in the summer of 1970/71, he was treated harshly by the press. They asserted that New South Wales wicketkeeper Brian Taber should have been given the job. However, it wasn't long before the talented keeper and hard-hitting batsman won over the skeptics with some brilliant performances. His association with D.K.Lillee (caught Marsh, bowled Lillee) was recorded 95 times in Tests, and those who saw them in action will never forget the sight of the thick-set keeper taking the great fast bowlers thunderbolts.

RIGHT That devastating style of Dennis Lillee in action, bowling for Western Australia. South Australia's captain, Ian Chappell is also pictured.

Index

368

The Australian XI 1905
J. J. Kelly
Frank Laver
J. Darling
Syd Gregory
Clem Hill
Warwick W. Armstrong